ASSESSING
English Language
Learners

Dedication

To TJG and GHG
The loves of my life

Margo Gottlieb

ASSESSING
English Language
Learners

Bridges From Language Proficiency to Academic Achievement

Foreword by Else Hamayan

CORWIN PRESS
A SAGE Publications Company
Thousand Oaks, California

For information:

Corwin Press
A Sage Publications Company
2455 Teller Road
Thousand Oaks, California 91320
www.corwinpress.com

Sage Publications Ltd.
1 Oliver's Yard
55 City Road
London EC1Y 1SP
United Kingdom

Sage Publications India Pvt. Ltd.
B-42 Panchsheel Enclave
Post Box 4109
New Delhi 110 017 India

Printed in the United States of America.

Library of Congress Cataloging-in-Publication Data

Gottlieb, Margo H.
Assessing English language learners : bridges from language
proficiency to academic achievement / Margo Gottlieb.
      p. cm.
Includes bibliographical references and index.
ISBN 978-0-7619-8888-5 (cloth : acid-free paper) — ISBN 978-0-7619-8889-2
(pbk. : acid-free paper)
   1. English language—Study and teaching—Foreign speakers. 2. English language—Ability testing. I. Title.
PE1128.A2G657 2006
428'.0076—dc22

                                          2005022979

This book is printed on acid-free paper.

13 14 15 16 17   16 15 14 13 12 11 10

Acquiring Editor:	Rachel Livsey
Editorial Assistant:	Phyllis Cappello
Production Editor:	Lynnette Pennings
Typesetter:	C&M Digitals (P) Ltd.
Cover Designer:	Lisa Miller

Contents

Foreword   ix

Preface   xi

   Acknowledgments   xii

About the Author   xv

1. **Assessment of English Language Learners:**
    The Bridge to Educational Equity   1
    English Language Learners and Their Teachers   2
    Considerations in the Assessment of English Language Learners   6
    Identification of English Language Learners   6
    Purposes for the Assessment of English Language Learners   8
    An Assessment Framework for English Language Learners   8
    Large-Scale and Classroom Assessment   11
    Summary and Final Thoughts   12
    Appendix 1.1 A Decision Tree for the Identification
      and Placement of English Language Learners   15
    Appendix 1.2 A Sample Home Language Survey
      to Administer to Newly Enrolled Students   16
    Appendix 1.3 A Sample Oral Language Use Survey   17
    Appendix 1.4 A Sample Literacy Survey for
      English Language Learners   18
    Appendix 1.5 Purposes for Classroom Assessment,
      Types of Measures, and Language of Assessment   19
    Appendix 1.6 An Assessment Framework for
      English Language Learners   20
    Appendix 1.7 A Schedule for Assessing English Language Learners   21
    Appendix 1.8 An Inventory of State, School-District, or
      School-Based Assessment Measures for English Language Learners   22

2. **Standards and Assessment: The Bridge From Language**
    Proficiency to Academic Achievement   23
    The Relationship Among Social Language Proficiency,
      Academic Language Proficiency, and Academic Achievement   24
    The Second-Language Acquisition Process   26
    Language Proficiency and Academic Content Standards   29

Summary and Final Thoughts   36

Appendix 2.1 REFLECTION: Comparing Targets for
    Language Proficiency and Academic Achievement   38

Appendix 2.2 Grouping English Language Learners by
    Levels of Language Proficiency   39

Appendix 2.3 A Checklist for Evaluating English
    Language Proficiency Standards   40

**3. Assessing Oral Language and Literacy
Development: The Bridge From Social Language
Proficiency to Academic Language Proficiency**   **41**

Language Proficiency Assessment: Oral Language   42

Language Proficiency Assessment: Literacy   49

Summary and Final Thoughts   58

Appendix 3.1 REFLECTION: Connections Between
    Oral Language and Literacy   59

Appendix 3.2 A Checklist for Analyzing Features of Large-Scale
    Language Proficiency Tests   60

**4. Assessing Academic Language Proficiency and Academic
Achievement: The Bridge to Accountability**   **63**

Content-Based Instruction and Assessment   64

Assessing Language and Content   65

Summary and Final Thoughts   80

Appendix 4.1 Features Associated With Assessment of
    Language and Content Across the Curriculum   81

Appendix 4.2 A Sample Listening Assessment Activity
    for Young English Language Learners   82

Appendix 4.3 REFLECTION: Multiple Meanings   83

5. Classroom Assessment: The Bridge to Educational Parity   **85**

The Distinctions Between Testing, Assessment, and Evaluation   85

Implementing Classroom Assessment   86

Summary and Final Thoughts   97

Appendix 5.1 The Measurement of
    English Language Proficiency and Academic Achievement
    at the Classroom and Large-Scale Levels   99

Appendix 5.2 REFLECTION: Questions, Activities, Tasks, or Projects   100

Appendix 5.3 The Parameters of Classroom Assessment   101

Appendix 5.4 A Review Sheet for Instructional Assessment
    Projects and Tasks for English Language Learners   102

Appendix 5.5 A Template for a Classroom Instructional
    Assessment Project   103

Appendix 5.6 A Completed Template for a Classroom
    Instructional Assessment Project   105

Appendix 5.7 Summary of Grading and Reporting
    Task 1 of the Weather Around the World Project   109

6. **Documenting Performance Assessment:**
   The Bridge From Teachers to Classrooms **111**
   Rationale for Performance Assessment for
       English Language Learners 111
   The Nature of Performance Assessment 112
   The Importance of Performance Assessment
       for English Language Learners 113
   The Role of Rubrics in Performance Assessment 114
   Overall Features of Rubrics 123
   Summary and Final Thoughts 123
   Appendix 6.1 REFLECTION: Matching
       Instruction to Assessment 126
   Appendix 6.2 REFLECTION: Possible Types of Rubrics
       for Matching Instruction to Assessment 127
   Appendix 6.3 An Interdisciplinary Project for Middle
       School English Language Learners:
       "Managing the Budget" 128
   Appendix 6.4 A Checklist of Rubric Features for
       English Language Learners 131

7. **Supports for Student, Classroom, and Large-Scale**
   Assessment: The Bridge to Student Understanding **133**
   Use of Visual or Graphic Support 134
   Cross-Cutting Instructional Assessment Techniques 138
   Continuity of Support From the Classroom to
       a Large-Scale Level 140
   Student Self-Assessment 141
   Large-Scale Student Self-Assessment 147
   Summary and Final Thoughts 147
   Appendix 7.1 Features of Graphic Organizers for
       English Language Learners 148
   Appendix 7.2 REFLECTION: Features of Classroom
       and Large-Scale Assessment 149

8. **Standardized Testing and Reporting:**
   The Bridge to Fair and Valid Assessment **151**
   Standardized Testing 152
   Standardized Testing and English Language Learners 155
   Summary and Final Thoughts 164
   Appendix 8.1 The Pluses and Minuses of Using
       Different Types of Scores From Norm-Referenced
       Standardized Achievement Tests 166
   Appendix 8.2 Comparison of Features of
       Standardized English Language Proficiency
       Tests Pre/Post the No Child Left Behind Act of 2001 167

9. **Grading Systems: The Bridge to the Future**   **169**

    The Issue of Grading   169

    Using Student Portfolios for Assessment and Grading   175

    Summary and Final Thoughts   182

    Appendix 9.1 An Assessment Portfolio Checklist   183

Glossary   **185**

References   **191**

Index   **197**

Foreword

Lately, it seems as though whenever a group of educators get together, the topic of assessment comes up. As high-stakes testing takes a bigger and bigger hold in schools, frustration with issues of assessment is rampant, especially for English language learners. With the passage of No Child Left Behind, stringent demands have been placed on educators. Assessment of English language learners has become a monster that troubles many who have fought battles in advocating for this group of students.

For those of us who tread gingerly into the world of assessment of English language learners, it also seems that taking on such a topic in a book is tantamount to foolish bravery. I have known Margo Gottlieb for many years, and I know that she is neither foolish nor does she have to be brave in taking on this task. She is well qualified to guide us through this maze. A deep understanding of the needs of English language learners is what makes her sensible research-based approach to assessment of these students unique. This understanding is enriched by a sensitivity to the plight of many English language learners in U.S. schools and a passion to attain a good education for them.

This book is written from the perspective of one who has spent a great many years and much energy thinking about English language learners. The author's commitment to English language learners is evidenced in a statement in the preface where she attributes a paradigm shift in the field of educational assessment to two great forces: the undeniable increase of language minority students and the treatment of English language learners in federal legislation. I am a little more cynical than to think that English language learners are in the forefront of mainstream educators' minds and the policies of the department of education at the federal level. However, I am comforted by the knowledge that this book is written by someone whose periscope has been focused primarily, if not solely, on English language learners.

Four things make this book particularly useful for me. First, it places the assessment of English language learners in the larger context of current-day educational assessment, with all its political and social considerations. Many schools have suffered the consequences of limited or invalid assessments erroneously depicting English language learners as not attaining the standards and expectations set for them. This has happened because of unnecessarily strict interpretation of federal laws, invalid testing, or invalid interpretation of test results. *Assessing English Language Learners: Bridges From Language Proficiency to Academic Achievement* provides assessment tools to avoid these pitfalls.

Second, every aspect of this book is based on the distinction between language proficiency and academic achievement. This distinction is a difficult one to make for many who are not well versed in second-language acquisition, bilingual proficiency, and the education of English language learners. Yet as Margo has said on so many occasions and to so many people, without thinking clearly about this distinction and understanding it, we cannot assess English language learners in a valid way. In her methodical and precise way, the author helps us understand not only the importance of this distinction but its essence.

Third, this book provides us with tools for producing, interpreting, and reporting reliable and valid data for educational decision making. The "Reflection" sections in each chapter are an added bonus whose purpose is to offer opportunities for readers to apply the discussion surrounding the instruction and assessment of English language learners to their own setting.

Finally, this book makes the solid relationship between instruction and assessment one of the tenets of sound educational decision making. I cannot emphasize enough how important this is. In this day and age, when testing takes up such a significant amount of class time, it is essential that teachers complete their assessments while they are instructing. I am amazed that large numbers of teachers still "stop teaching" in order to assess their students. This book defines instruction as one of the crucial elements of a good assessment, where evidence of performance and knowledge attainment is systematically gathered, organized, and analyzed. Most impressive is that it includes suggestions for ways to incorporate instruction into even large-scale assessment.

In my career in English language learner education, I have learned a great deal from my colleague, Margo Gottlieb. It is fortunate that she has decided to share the wealth of her knowledge, wisdom, and experience regarding the assessment of English language learners with a wider audience. Each chapter of this book begins with a quotation; I will end this foreword with the quotation that begins Chapter 6: *I have not been by that bridge . . . without yearning to cross it.* Assessment is not a bridge that many of us yearn to cross. Yet this book makes assessment such a bridge. With all the offerings that Margo Gottlieb provides in this book, she makes us yearn not only to cross the bridge of assessment but to feel confident when we get to the other side.

Else Hamayan
Illinois Resource Center
Des Plaines, Illinois

Preface

In his seminal book, *The Structure of Scientific Revolutions* (1962), Thomas Kuhn envisions a paradigm shift as the point in time when an overwhelming mass of accumulated knowledge reaches a critical point that forces us to adjust our way of thinking. The United States is currently undergoing such a paradigm shift in the field of educational assessment. The momentum behind this rethinking has been spurred by two forces: (1) the undeniable, exponential increase of language minority students in our K-12 education system and (2) the treatment of English language learners, a subset of the linguistically and culturally diverse student population, in research, practice, and federal legislation.

Assessing English Language Learners: Bridges From Language Proficiency to Academic Achievement is organized around the linkages or bridges that span the competing paradigms currently in flux in assessment. Each chapter highlights a bridge that educators must cross and illustrates how theory and practice are undergoing change. In doing so, it discusses critical issues and offers practical suggestions on how to approach assessment for English language learners.

The first two chapters set the background for this paradigm shift. Chapter 1, "Assessment of English Language Learners: The Bridge to Educational Equity," paints the assessment landscape by identifying its key players, the students and their teachers. It describes an assessment framework for English language learners, the purposes of assessment, and the types of measures in large-scale and classroom contexts. Chapter 2, "Standards and Assessment: The Bridge From Language Proficiency to Academic Achievement," discusses the influence of two languages in shaping the language proficiency, academic proficiency, and academic achievement of English language learners. It then characterizes the second language acquisition process as passage through a series of scaffolded levels of language proficiency. Last, it illustrates how English language proficiency and academic content standards are the anchor and stimuli for educational reform of English language learners.

The body of the book addresses how English language learners are to be involved in large-scale and classroom assessment. In Chapter 3, "Assessing Oral Language and Literacy Development: The Bridge From Social Language Proficiency to Academic Language Proficiency," we examine each language domain: listening, speaking, reading, and writing. Chapter 4, "Assessing Academic Language Proficiency and Academic Achievement: The Bridge to Accountability," offers ideas in how to differentiate instruction and assessment in the core curricular areas of math, science, and social studies. Chapter 5, "Classroom Assessment: The Bridge to Educational Parity," provides an organization scheme for planning and delivering classroom assessment along with a sample project.

The last chapters concentrate on documentation, reporting, and interpretation of assessment results. Chapter 6, "Documenting Performance Assessment: The Bridge from Teachers to Classrooms," demonstrates how standards-based performance measures can complement standardized tools for English language learners. The sample rubrics provide a rich array of choices for teachers in how to interpret student work. Chapter 7, "Supports for Student, Classroom, and Large-Scale Assessment: The Bridge to Student Understanding," offers strategies for promoting content-based instruction through visual or graphic support. It carries the voice of our learners and how, through self-assessment and reflection, our students contribute to the assessment process.

We couldn't have written an assessment book without addressing the impact of standardized testing, the subject of Chapter 8, "Standardized Testing and Reporting: The Bridge to Fair and Valid Assessment." It treats how results from standardized measures are reported and how educators can use the data. The last chapter, "Grading Systems: The Bridge to the Future," proposes a set of fair grading practices for English language learners and how it translates into a standards-based report card.

Bridges are the pathways to educational success for English language learners. In this transition to a new educational paradigm, we face a multitude of challenges. The accomplishments of current and future generations of students rest on teachers forging new ground today. . . . *Assessing English Language Learners* provides teachers with the tools to do that.

ACKNOWLEDGMENTS

Many persons have devoted much time and effort in making this book a reality. Rachel Livsey, senior acquisitions editor, has coordinated this undertaking and has offered advice, comments, and encouragement on the earliest draft. Phyllis Cappello, senior editorial assistant, has provided guidelines and has answered the many queries along the way. Lynnette Pennings, production editor, and Linda Gray, copy editor, have refined the manuscript in preparation for publication. This note of gratitude extends to all those involved in the process.

The contributions of the following reviewers are gratefully acknowledged:

J. Sabrina Mims
Professor of Education
California State University, Los Angeles
Los Angeles, CA

Margarita Calderón
Research Scientist
Johns Hopkins University
Baltimore, MD

Cynthia Chew Nations
Senior Consultant
Teachscape/Learning 24–7
El Paso, TX

About the Author

Margo Gottlieb is a specialist in the design of assessments for English language learners in PreK–12 settings and in the evaluation of educational programs. Having started her career as an English as a second language (ESL) and bilingual teacher, for the past two decades, Margo has consulted with and provided technical assistance to governments, states, school districts, publishers, universities, and professional organizations. In 2004, Margo was a Fulbright Scholar, serving as a Senior Specialist in Chile and an evaluator for a dual-language school in Italy; in 2002, she was a teacher educator in Brazil. She has served on numerous U.S. and state task forces, advisory committees, and expert panels in addition to presenting at over a 100 international and national conferences.

Presently, Margo is Director, Assessment and Evaluation, Illinois Resource Center, and Lead Developer for World-Class Instructional Design and Assessment (WIDA), a multistate consortium. Active in Teachers of English to Speakers of Other Languages (TESOL), a global education association, she currently chairs the committee on the PreK–12 English language proficiency standards and has held numerous leadership positions.

Margo's degrees include a PhD in public policy analysis, evaluation research, and program design, an MA in applied linguistics, and a BA in the teaching of Spanish. She has published a host of assessment instruments, manuals, guidebooks, monographs, chapters, technical reports, and articles. In addition, she is a contributing author to a comprehensive K–5 ESL program.

Assessment of English Language Learners

The Bridge to Educational Equity

Challenges are gifts that force us to search for a new center of gravity. Don't fight them. Just find a different way to stand.

—Oprah Winfrey

As educators, we are constantly challenged to make informed decisions about our students; to do so, we plan, gather, and analyze information from multiple sources over time so that the results are meaningful to teaching and learning. That's the core of the **assessment** process and the centerpiece in the education of linguistically and culturally diverse students. If reliable, valid, and fair for our students, assessment can be the bridge to educational equity.

In this chapter, we begin laying the groundwork for assessment equity by defining the ever-increasing student population known as English language learners, their unique characteristics, and the teachers with whom they work. Next, the purposes for assessment are mapped onto an organizing framework. Finally, the distinction between **large-scale** and **classroom assessment** leads teachers to create a framework for their implementation with English language learners.

ENGLISH LANGUAGE LEARNERS AND THEIR TEACHERS

During the past decade, the staggering growth in the numbers of students with diverse languages and cultures across the United States has affected teachers and administrators from preschool through high school and beyond. This heterogeneous mix of students has had very different life and educational experiences; some are refugees, others are immigrants, still others have been born and raised here. The following is a synopsis of some of the major changes in our student population over the past decade.

The Demographics of Our Schools

There is an increased presence of linguistically and culturally diverse students, in general, and English language learners, in particular, in our schools throughout the nation. Here is a thumbnail sketch of the some facts and figures about this unique group of students.

- As of the 2002–2003 academic year, the 5,000,000 plus **English language learners** in public schools represented approximately 10% of the total pre-kindergarten (Pre-K) through Grade 12 enrollment.
- From 1993 to 2003, the growth of English language learners in elementary and secondary schools was 84% in relation to the 14% rise by the general student population.
- The greatest numbers of our English language learners live in California, with over 1.6 million; however, each of five other states has more than 125,000 identified English language learners: Arizona, Florida, Illinois, New York, and Texas.
- Nineteen states have witnessed a more than 200% growth in their English language learner population this past decade, many of which had not previously been affected by these changing demographics (National Clearinghouse for English Language Acquisition).
- There is a heavier concentration of younger English language learners, with 67% of these learners being at the elementary school level.
- Nationwide, the top 5 of the 240 reported languages, along with their percentage of the total, are as follows: Spanish (79.2 %), Vietnamese (2%), Hmong (1.6%), Cantonese (1%), and Korean (1%), with 19 additional languages spoken by more than 10,000 students (Kindler, 2002).
- Latinos or Hispanics are officially the largest minority group in the United States with 38.8 million residents, as confirmed by the U.S. Census Bureau in June 2003.
- The July 2003 update of the 2000 census reveals a continued surge in the Hispanic population, with an increase of 9.8%, followed by a 9% increase in the number of Asians. In contrast, the general U.S. population has grown at a rate of 2.5% during the same time period (El Nassar, 2003).

The linguistically and culturally diverse student population is on the rise and so too are the numbers of teachers who work with these students each day. Not all linguistically and culturally diverse students, however, are English language learners. So before we begin our journey into the world of assessment, we first need a clear definition of this important subgroup of students.

A Definition of English Language Learners

Any school-aged child exposed to a culture and language, other than English, in daily interaction in his or her home environment is considered a linguistically and culturally diverse student. English language learners are a subgroup of these students, who have been identified, through assessment, as having levels of English **language proficiency** and academic achievement that preclude them from accessing, processing, and acquiring unmodified grade-level material in English. Until recently, the term *limited English proficient* was assigned to this group of students; for the most part, the remnant of this label is found only in federal legislation. Generally, the education community refers to the linguistically and culturally diverse students qualified for support services as *English language learners,* the term used in this book.

The federal government has contributed to the national conversation regarding the definition of English language learners. Title IX of the No Child Left Behind Act (the Elementary and Secondary School Act of 2001) sets some general parameters for defining these students. State criteria for identifying English language learners are more directly related to school performance, refining the federal definition.

Criteria for eligibility are often bound to assessment results. Student scores on a variety of tools with proven **reliability** and **validity** determine whether students meet the qualifications to be considered English language learners. Measures may include the following:

1. Standardized English language proficiency **tests**, anchored in state English **language proficiency standards**

2. **Standardized test**s of academic achievement in language arts, mathematics, science, and optionally, social studies, with **accommodations** for English language learners, based on **academic content standards**

3. State academic assessments or systems designed for English language learners with statewide mechanisms (in the form of **rubrics** or scoring guides) for reporting classroom-based data on language proficiency and academic achievement (in English and the **native language**, as applicable)

Initial identification and placement of English language learners generally occur at a district intake center or neighborhood school. School districts with large concentrations of linguistically and culturally diverse students may afford an assessment specialist; otherwise, teachers with specific training in **English as a second language** (ESL) or **bilingual education** should be involved in the initial assessment process. Once students are identified as English language learners and assigned to a classroom, teachers need to collaborate to create a coordinated assessment and instructional plan.

The Teachers Who Work With English Language Learners

All teachers within a school should take responsibility for the education of English language learners, and many may work with these students on a daily basis. Figure 1.1 illustrates one such configuration, typical of elementary schools, where most activities center on the classroom or homeroom teacher. This flower-shaped organizational design may also apply to high schools; in this case, the centerpiece would be the students' base teacher with each of their content teachers constituting the petals.

The education of English language learners rests with all teachers in a school. As depicted in Figure 1.1, each teacher has a distinct and complementary role to ensure that students have maximum access to rigorous and challenging curriculum, instruction, and assessment. Table 1.1 describes the overall responsibilities of these teachers, each of whom contributes to the total educational program of our students.

In schools where students are afforded instruction in their native language (**L1**), bilingual or dual-language teachers introduce, reinforce, and assess the skills and knowledge of the core content areas (language arts/reading, mathematics, science, and social studies). By integrating native language and content, English language learners develop a strong foundation in oral language and literacy that will readily transfer to English.

ESL teachers (who have other labels in different regions of the U.S.), introduce, reinforce, and assess the language patterns and vocabulary associated with schooling and the core content areas. Implementing a content-based curriculum in English, they preview the concepts that the English language learners will encounter in the general education classroom. If students qualify for Title I, and services are offered, these teachers may assist in extending the literacy and math skills of English language learners either in their native language or in English. Likewise, the physical

Figure 1.1   The Network of Teachers Who Might Work With English Language Learners

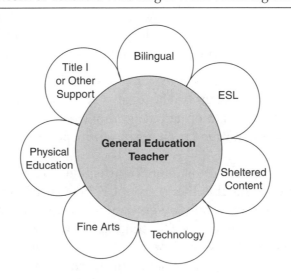

education, fine arts, and other resource teachers, including special education (for students with disabilities), support students' language development throughout the time they are acquiring a second language.

Classroom teachers often coordinate the English language learners' educational activities to ensure their continuity of services and a cohesive, well-articulated instructional assessment program. Their focus is on literacy instruction in English (in concert with native language literacy) as well as promoting conceptual understanding within the content areas.

In each chapter, you will encounter a reflection or two. Their purpose is to offer opportunities for you to apply some of the issues surrounding the instruction and assessment of English language learners to your own setting. These reflections are meant to be shared with colleagues to gain multiple perspectives on how to approach the challenges facing teachers. Here is the first one.

REFLECTION: Teachers Working With English Language Learners

Think about all the teachers in your school or district who are responsible for the education of English language learners. Using Figure 1.1 as a model, make a chart or diagram that reflects how they work together in providing services to students. Then describe your figure along with the roles and responsibilities of each teacher.

Table1.1   Primary Responsibilities of Teachers Who Might Work With English Language Learners

Teacher(s)	Instruction and Assessment Responsibilities
Bilingual	• Native language (L1) academic support • Oral language and literacy development in L1
English as a second language (ESL)	• Language development in English (L2) • Introduction/reinforcement of concepts in L2
Sheltered content	• Language and conceptual development in English (L2) • Content specific skills and knowledge in L2
Title I or other support	• Literacy reinforcement in L1 or L2 • Reinforcement of math skills and knowledge
General Education	• Literacy development in L2 • Academic development in L2
Specials (technology, fine arts, physical education)	• Extension of language and skill development in L2 (and L1, as applicable)

SOURCE: Adapted from Gottlieb and Nguyen (2004).

CONSIDERATIONS IN THE ASSESSMENT OF ENGLISH LANGUAGE LEARNERS

English language learners are a national resource that adds to the richness of our schools. A careful examination of the unique characteristics of English language learners helps teachers understand how language, culture, and prior experiences shape the identities of these diverse students. Table 1.2 identifies the factors that must be taken into account in the instruction and assessment of English language learners.

Not all data on English language learners necessary for decision making come from assessment tools. Information pertaining to students' mobility, continuity in education, types of support services, the amount of time devoted to support per week, and the language(s) of instruction over the years can be obtained through background surveys as part of school registration (see Appendices 1.3 and 1.4, at the end of this chapter, for examples). Teachers can use this survey information, in conjunction with assessment data, as a starting point for instruction and classroom assessment.

Table 1.2   Variables That Influence the Academic Success of English Language Learners

- The language(s) and culture(s) of everyday interaction
- The exposure to academic language outside school
- Educational experiences outside and in the United States
- Continuity of educational experiences (mobility, interruption of schooling)
- Proficiency (including literacy) in the native language (L1)
- Academic achievement in the native language
- Proficiency (including literacy) in English (L2)
- Academic achievement in English
- Allotment of time per day for educational support services
- Amount and type of sustained support across years—stability of instructional program and language(s) of delivery
- Socioeconomic status in the United States, including access to resources and opportunities for learning

IDENTIFICATION OF ENGLISH LANGUAGE LEARNERS

The initial assessment process, outlined in the flowchart in Appendix 1.1, begins when any student walks through the school doors for the first time. The **Home Language Survey** (see Appendix 1.2), incorporated into the initial registration process, serves to differentiate monolingual English-speaking students from those who interact in another language and culture on a daily basis. Once students are known to have come from linguistically and culturally diverse backgrounds, further screening is required. In this first round of assessment, Tier I measures include the following:

1. Survey of oral language use (optional)

2. Literacy survey (optional)

3. Standards-based, reliable, and valid screener (test) of English language proficiency

Based on results from these and other state or district requirements, teachers—or in some cases, assessment specialists—determine if students qualify as English language learners and are eligible for support services. If so, more diagnostic information can then be obtained from a set of Tier II measures.

Tier I Measures

Tier I measures provide an overall picture of students. The Home Language Survey, required by most states, serves as an initial screening device and should be made available in the students' and families' native language. A YES response to any of the questions, such as, "Does the child speak a language other than English?" triggers the subsequent administration of an English language proficiency test and optional language surveys (see Appendices 1.3 and 1.4).

Student language surveys, although not required, provide teachers insight into students' language use and literacy practices. Even though there is always caution in interpreting self-reported results, this information is invaluable in gaining insight into students' educational backgrounds and experiences. School districts or schools should translate these surveys so that they are available in the languages of the student body. Otherwise, paraprofessionals or bilingual student buddies might be helpful in translating and obtaining the information.

An English language proficiency test, approved or issued by the state, serves as the primary tool for identification of English language learners. On the basis of results for listening, speaking, reading, writing, and comprehension, students are assigned a level of English language proficiency. Those students who qualify as English language learners may then be further assessed with Tier II measures, a school or district choice, to best match students with the most appropriate and effective instructional program.

Tier II Measures

Tier II measures complement Tier I measures by offering more specific information. They center on students' academic achievement (in L1 and L2) and may include standardized tests, informal reading inventories, and content-based writing samples. Although instruction may or may not be afforded in the students' native language, assessment in L1 is of utmost importance for students new to a school district.

There are several reasons for suggesting native language assessment at the time of initial identification of English language learners when instruction is offered only in English. First, English language learners are a heterogeneous mix of students with different proficiencies, literacies, knowledge bases, and school experiences. Second, achievement in L1 is the strongest predictor of future success in L2 (Thomas & Collier, 2002). This information is invaluable for teachers in planning and delivering instruction. Students with strong conceptual development in L1 merely need to acquire the labels for the concepts they already know; conversely, students without such a foundation may need to learn both literacy and content simultaneously. Instructional methodologies and the type of support services vary considerably for these two broad categories of students.

Student data on academic achievement pinpoint placement and provide diagnostic information for teachers. This information, coupled with that from language proficiency testing and survey results, establishes the basis for selection of an optimal program design and services for English language learners. In addition, teachers have a firm sense of how to plan sound instruction and assessment.

PURPOSES FOR THE ASSESSMENT OF ENGLISH LANGUAGE LEARNERS

Unless educators know why we assess English language learners, there is bound to be misinterpretation of the data. As outlined in Table 1.3, generally, there are five major purposes for assessment of English language learners. Classroom teachers are directly involved in the ongoing monitoring of student performance (the second purpose in the table). Although the other purposes of assessment may be peripheral to day-to-day instruction, teachers may provide input for decision making and should be informed of any and all results that affect their classrooms or students.

Teachers working with English language learners need to have a sense of the students' baseline or starting point for both language proficiency and academic achievement in order to document their progress over time, either from initial placement or information from previous teachers. Classroom assessments that mirror instructional practices and the language(s) of instruction provide day-to-day feedback. Standard student portfolios, where a uniform set of original student work is collected and analyzed, offer another form of evidence of student performance.

Besides the primary purposes for assessment, classroom data on our students are necessary for other reasons. The reflection in Appendix 1.5 asks teachers to think about the most appropriate tools for assessing English language learners. Irrespective of the purposes, teachers are to base their decisions on multiple criteria and assessments.

AN ASSESSMENT FRAMEWORK FOR ENGLISH LANGUAGE LEARNERS

Assessment of English language learners is a more complex undertaking than assessment of proficient English-speaking students because it involves the documentation of both language proficiency and academic achievement. Language proficiency is an expression of students' linguistic knowledge and language use in four

Table 1.3 The Primary Purposes for Assessing English Language Learners and Their Associated Types of Measures

Purposes for Student Assessment	Types of Measures—Use of Multiple Criteria for Decision Making
Identification and placement to determine eligibility for support services	• Home Language Survey • Additional language surveys and records (e.g., transcripts) • Standardized English language proficiency test(s) • Measures of academic achievement in L1 and L2
Monitoring progress of English language proficiency and academic achievement	• Classroom assessments that reflect the language(s) of instruction • Standard student portfolios, including student self-assessment • District- or school-level measures
Accountability for English language proficiency and academic achievement	• State assessment/alternate assessment for academic achievement • State English language proficiency test • District-level measures of academic achievement in L1 and L2
Reclassification within or transition from support services	• Accountability measures • Standard student portfolios, including student self-assessment • Teacher recommendations based on classroom assessments and other data (e.g., GPAs)
Program evaluation to ascertain effectiveness of support services	• Contextual variables (e.g., demographics, types of support services) • Accountability measures • Standard student portfolios, including student self-assessment

language domains; listening, speaking, reading, and writing. In the traditional sense, language proficiency entails contexts and interactions in and outside of school; thus language competence or ability represents the acquisition of language regardless of how, where, or under what conditions (Bachman, 1990). In contrast, academic achievement reflects students' subject matter knowledge, skills, and concepts across the core content areas (language arts, mathematics, science, and social studies). It is a mark of conceptual learning directly tied to school-based curriculum and, in recent times, state academic content standards (Gottlieb, 2003).

Language proficiency and academic achievement measures used with English language learners can be plotted onto an assessment framework. Each teacher of English language learners completes the portions that apply so that all teachers will have a sense of the extent and range of assessment for these students. Table 1.4 provides a sample assessment framework; a blank form can be found in Appendix 1.6 for individual use.

Table 1.4   A Sample Assessment Framework for English Language Learners

	Language Proficiency				Academic Achievement			
	Listening	*Speaking*	*Reading*	*Writing*	*Language Arts*	*Mathematics*	*Science*	*Social Studies*
Assessment Measures	State test of English language proficiency				State assessment of academic achievement in English or alternate assessments for English language learners in L2 or L1			
					District measures for English language learners in L2 or L1			
	Teacher observation Interviews or student-led conferences		Leveled readers for ESL	Journals Writing samples	Informal reading inventories	Raw math problems	Observation during science experiments	Dramatization of historical events
	Interdisciplinary, thematic projects with language proficiency and academic achievement rubrics							
Teacher(s) Responsible								

SOURCE: Adapted from Gottlieb and Nguyen (2004).

LARGE-SCALE AND CLASSROOM ASSESSMENT

In schools, a distinction is made between large-scale and classroom assessment. Large-scale assessment refers to the use of standard conditions across multiple classrooms, including departments or grade levels, schools, school districts, or states in the planning, gathering, analyzing, and reporting of student data (Gottlieb, 2003). Classroom assessment involves the documentation of student performance that is planned, collected, and interpreted by teachers as part of the instructional cycle. Standardized, norm-referenced tests fall under the large-scale classification, whereas journal writing, for example, qualifies as a classroom measure. A comparison of the features of large-scale and classroom measures is presented in Table 1.5.

A variety of assessment tools can be classified as either large-scale or classroom-based. The primary distinction is that large-scale measures are either standard in their administration or are standardized tools; that is, teachers must use the identical set of procedures for data collection, analysis, scoring, and reporting. Classroom measures, on the other hand, are more flexible in use. Examples of these two types of assessment measures are listed in Table 1.6.

The language of assessment may vary within large-scale or classroom contexts. State assessment, for example, may be exclusively in English. However, in dual-language or language enrichment classrooms, assessment proceeds in two languages for both English language learners and proficient English speakers. The allocation of language (either L1 or L2) for instruction is mirrored in assessment. Where English language learners are not afforded support in their native language, assessment, as instruction, should be modified and given in English.

Table 1.5 The Features of Large-Scale and Classroom Assessment

Large-Scale Measures	Classroom Measures
Summative in nature, occurring at designated time intervals, at the same month each year (such as state assessment)	Formative in nature, occurring on an ongoing basis, such as every week
Standardized or standard in their administration; teachers all read and follow the same set of directions and procedures, for example	Individualized for classrooms or students, such as a sixth-grade math test
Designed and implemented at department, program, district, or state levels (such as end-of-course test)	Teacher created; teachers construct and score the measures
Generally restricted to testing, such as multiple-choice and short-answer questions	Use of a variety of approaches and response formats where students produce original work
Within a designated time frame, such as over several class periods	Within an extended time frame, such as projects or units of instruction

Table 1.6   Types of Large-Scale and Classroom Measures

Large-Scale Measures	Classroom Measures
State tests	Informal reading inventories
District assessments, such as norm-referenced or criterion-referenced tests, writing samples, or other performance tasks with their accompanying standard rubrics	Structured observation
	Extended projects with descriptors or criteria
	End-of-unit tests
Program-based assessments	Performance tasks (e.g., writing samples, speeches, exhibits, demonstrations) with specific criteria or rubrics
End-of-course tests	
Department-level tests	Student portfolios and rubrics
Standard portfolios and rubrics	Interviews and conferences
	Student self-assessment

An Assessment Plan

Teachers should have a plan to deal with all the assessments that occur during the school year. Table 1.7, a schedule for assessment of English language learners, provides a sample month-by-month account of large-scale and classroom measures. (A blank schedule can be found in Appendix 1.7). Depending on the context of instruction, the rows may be subdivided to differentiate assessment of English language proficiency from that of academic achievement. It may be helpful for teachers who work with English language learners to share the information or jointly complete a schedule to avoid overburdening students with assessments.

In this schedule, the dates for large-scale assessments, which are usually fixed, should be entered first. Next, teachers should collectively decide what data are most useful for evaluating students on a quarterly, trimester, or semester basis, depending on when report cards are issued. Classroom times for assessment should be selected to complement those required of large-scale measures.

Multiple measures of English language learners' oral language, literacy, and conceptual development should be collected throughout the year. If more than one language is used for instruction, the schedule also serves as a cross-check to ensure a match with assessment. Ready to begin instruction and assessment of English language learners, teachers will be introduced to language proficiency and academic content standards in the next chapter.

SUMMARY AND FINAL THOUGHTS

The growing presence of English language learners in our classrooms and the tightening of school, district, and state accountability give reason to reexamine the assessment measures we use. Appendix 1.8 is a list of measures appropriate for the

Table 1.7   A Hypothetical Schedule for Assessing English Language Learners

	August	September	October	November	December	January	February	March	April	May	June
Language(s)	L2 (and L1)		L2 (and L1)	L2 (and L1)		L2 (and L1)			L2 (and L1)	L2 (and L1)	L2 (and L1)
Classroom assessment measures	Reading and math placements		Writing sample	Content area logs and projects		Student-led conferences			Content area logs and projects	Oral language samples	Student portfolios
Language(s)		L2					L2 (and L1)	L2 (and L1)			
Large-scale assessment measures		State English language proficiency test					District writing sample	State assessment of academic achievement			

SOURCE: TESOL, Atlantic Academy, Washington, D.C.

assessment of English language learners mentioned in this chapter. Teachers need to be aware of the many forms of assessment, whether large scale or classroom based, our students encounter while in school.

Assessment is not an isolated activity but a component of a system. One such system for English language learners is illustrated in Figure 1.2. The paired components of this system can be considered gears that work in an interlocking, coordinated fashion. Anchored in language proficiency and academic content standards, large-scale and classroom measures influence curriculum and instruction.

Assessment of English language learners must be inclusive, fair, relevant, comprehensive, valid and yield meaningful information. Teachers must understand the power of assessment data in helping us provide the evidence that our students are learning and making progress. Ultimately, it is our responsibility as educators to create a bridge, through sound assessment, to ensure the academic success of our English language learners.

Figure 1.2   Components of an Assessment System for English Language Learners

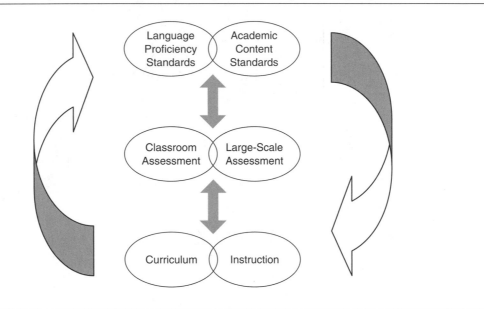

APPENDIX 1.1

A Decision Tree for the Identification and Placement of English Language Learners

Newly enrolled student in a state or school district

$\downarrow$

- Administer Home Language Survey

$\downarrow$

Linguistically and culturally diverse student? YES*

$\downarrow$

Proceed with Tier I measures
- Administer Oral Language Use Survey and Literacy Survey
- Administer English Language Proficiency Test

$\downarrow$

English language learner? YES

$\downarrow$

Proceed with Tier II measures
- Administer measures of Language Proficiency and Academic Achievement in Native Language (L1)**
- Administer measures of academic achievement in L2 (English)

$\downarrow$

Eligible for support services? YES
Place student in an educational program according to survey and test results

---

*At any point where the answer to the question is NO, students are placed in the **general education program**.

**Native language measures are recommended for initial entry and then annually, provided instruction is in L1.

APPENDIX 1.2

A Sample Home Language Survey to Administer to Newly Enrolled Students

Help us know about you. Please answer these questions.

Is a language other than English spoken in your home?

YES   NO

Which language? _____

Do you speak a language other than English with someone in your home?

YES   NO

Which language? _____

Do you speak a language other than English **every day** at home?

YES   NO

4. Put an X in the box on the top line to show the grades you went to school here in the United States. Put an X on the bottom line for the grades where you went to school in another country. Put a circle around the year(s) you did not go to school.

	Grade Level													
Schools in the U.S.	Pre-K	K	1	2	3	4	5	6	7	8	9	10	11	12
Schools outside the U.S.	Pre-K	K	1	2	3	4	5	6	7	8	9	10	11	12

APPENDIX 1.3

A Sample Oral Language Use Survey

Directions: I am going to ask you which language or languages you use around your home, neighborhood, and school. Tell me if you use your first (or native) language (L1), _____, English (L2), or both languages with the people and places that I name. *As the student responds, mark the designated box.*

	First or Native Language (L1)	Second Language, English (L2)	Both Languages (L1 + L2)	Not Applicable
Around Your Home				
With your parents or guardians				
With your grandparents				
With your brothers and sisters				
With other relatives who live with you				
With your caregivers (if any)				
With your neighbors				
With your friends				
Around Your Neighborhood				
At the store				
At the clinic or doctor's office				
At church (if applicable)				
Outside, as in a park				
At a restaurant or fast food place				
Around Your School				
On the playground or outside				
In the lunchroom				
In the halls				
During free time				

SOURCE: Adapted from Gottlieb, M., & Hamayan, E. (in press). Assessing language proficiency of English language learners in special education contexts. In G. B. Esquivel, E. C. Lopez, & S. Nahari (Eds.). *Handbook of multicultural school psychology.* New York: Lawrence Erlbaum.

APPENDIX 1.4

A Sample Literacy Survey for English Language Learners

Directions: Which kinds of materials do you read and write outside of school? Mark the box to show whether you use your first (or native) language (L1), _____, English (L2), or both languages when you read and write.

Before or after school . . .	First or Native Language (L1)	Second Language, English (L2)	Both Languages (L1 + L2)	Not Applicable
I Read				
Street signs and names				
Maps or directions				
Schedules (e.g., school bus or train)				
Newspapers				
Magazines				
Notes from friends, such as e-mails				
Information from the Internet				
Brochures/pamphlets				
Short stories				
Poetry				
Books				
I Write				
Information on papers or forms				
Lists				
Memos or notes				
E-mails				
Letters to family members or for school				
Short stories				
Poetry or songs				

SOURCE: Adapted from Gottlieb (1999a).

APPENDIX 1.5

REFLECTION: Purposes for Classroom Assessment, Types of Measures, and Language of Assessment

In this table, there is a list of possible types of measures associated with a purpose for classroom assessment of English language learners (those that do not fit are marked with an X). Based on your personal knowledge, or that of other teachers in your school, write the names of the measures that are used in the designated box. Then discuss with other teachers how you use the information obtained from assessment.

Purpose for Assessment: to Determine a Student's . . .	Types of Measures				Not Applicable
	Language Proficiency		Academic Achievement		
	Languages of administration				
	L1	L2	L1	L2	
Relative language proficiency (performance in one language in relation to a second one)			x	x	
Overall progress in English language acquisition	x		x	x	
Necessity for prereferral for evaluation for learning disabilities					
Diagnosis within a specific language domain, such as reading comprehension					
Eligibility of additional support services					
Depth of knowledge on a topic within a curricular area	x	x			

APPENDIX 1.6

An Assessment Framework for English Language Learners

	Language Proficiency				Academic Achievement			
	Listening	Speaking	Reading	Writing	Language Arts	Mathematics	Science	Social Studies
Assessment Measures	State test of English language proficiency				State assessment of academic achievement in English (or alternate assessments for English language learners in L2 or L1)			
Teacher(s) Responsible								

APPENDIX 1.7

A Schedule for Assessing English Language Learners

School year: _____

School district: _____

Teacher(s): _____

School: _____

Grade level: _____

Month	August	September	October	November	December	January	February	March	April	May	June	July
Language(s)												
Classroom assessment measures												
Language(s)												
Large-scale assessments measures												

APPENDIX 1.8

An Inventory of State, School-District, or School-Based Assessment Measures for English Language Learners

Here is a list of measures that your state, school district, or school may currently have in place for its English language learners. Take an inventory and put an X in the boxes alongside the measures present in your setting.

☐ A home language survey

☐ An oral language use survey

☐ A literacy survey

☐ A standards-based English language proficiency test

☐ A standards-based measure of academic achievement in L1

☐ A standards-based measure of academic achievement in L2 (English)

☐ Accommodations for state assessment for English language learners (provisions, such as extended time, that may enhance student performance but that do not affect the test's validity)

☐ Informal reading inventories

☐ Standard classroom measures, such as oral language or writing samples, along with scoring rubrics

2

Standards and Assessment

The Bridge From Language Proficiency to Academic Achievement

When you build bridges, you can keep crossing them.

—Rick Pitino

In the assessment framework for **English language learners**, we first differentiate **language proficiency** from **academic achievement**. The first section of this chapter clarifies these terms and their application to English language learners. By doing so, we start to construct the bridge from language proficiency to academic achievement for our students. The last part of the chapter addresses how standards help facilitate this connection.

THE RELATIONSHIP AMONG SOCIAL LANGUAGE PROFICIENCY, ACADEMIC LANGUAGE PROFICIENCY, AND ACADEMIC ACHIEVEMENT

Three concepts introduced in this section are interwoven throughout the book: **social language proficiency, academic language proficiency**, and academic achievement. Teachers are keenly aware of the importance of academic achievement for all students; however, they may not realize that language proficiency is of equal significance for second language learners. To be successful in school, English language learners must acquire both the social and the academic aspects of language as they are learning content.

Social and Academic Language Functions

Language proficiency represents an individual's competence or ability to use language regardless of how, where, or under what conditions it has been acquired (Bachman, 1990). It is associated with general linguistic knowledge, understanding, and use across the **language domains** of listening, speaking, reading, and writing. Another defining feature of language proficiency is its **language functions**, the ways in which language is used to communicate a message (Finocchiaro & Brumfit, 1983; Halliday, 1976).

Language proficiency reflects the acquisition of language inside and outside of school. However, in recent years, federal legislation, with its emphasis on standards-based academic performance, has narrowed the definition for English language learners. Thus while the social and cultural aspects of acquiring a language are to be respected, the academic aspects of language proficiency are most tied to schooling and accountability.

Language functions, descriptions of how students use language, can be both social and academic in nature. When language functions are associated with the social dimension of language proficiency, there is generally an implicit, underlying interaction with another person. Salutations, apologies, complaints, and requests, for example, represent social language behaviors. On the other hand, language functions descriptive of academic proficiency often interact with behaviors associated with cognition, such as categorization, interpretation, and justification.

English language learners must be exposed to and practice multiple and varied language functions within the school setting. Teachers have to remember that English language learners must simultaneously acclimate socially, acculturate to their school climate, and progress academically. Examples of how students use language in school according to their primary focus, either social or academic proficiency, are provided in Table 2.1.

Social and Academic Language Proficiency

The social dimensions of language proficiency are part of teachers' instructional routines and school life. Teachers may ask young students to raise their hands, get in

Table 2.1   A Sampling of Social and Academic Language Functions

Social Language Functions	Academic Language Functions
• Give and ask permission • Request assistance • Make introductions or salutations • Share feelings • Offer compliments • Apologize or express regret	• Defend a position or stance • Compare and contrast ideas, people, or events • Sequence processes, procedures, or operations • Debate issues or ideas • Summarize conflicts, story lines, or results of investigations

line, or bring notes to the office, whereas they expect older students to use the proper register when speaking with adults, assume a role in a cooperative group, or conduct class meetings. *Social* language proficiency, as it reflects everyday experiences, is acquired within the first years of interacting with a new language on a sustained basis.

However, it is *academic* language proficiency that drives content-based curriculum and instruction. Academic language proficiency refers to the language patterns and concepts required in processing, understanding, and communicating curriculum-based content. When English language learners are asked to rank modes of transportation by their speed, for example, they must know comparatives; that is, a car goes fast, an airplane goes faster, and a space shuttle goes the fastest. Academic language proficiency is a lengthy process and is often literacy dependent. As such, it may take more than a decade for some English language learners to reach that goal (Thomas & Collier, 2002).

Academic Language Proficiency and Academic Achievement

Academic language proficiency differs from academic achievement for English language learners. Academic language proficiency centers on the delivery or understanding of an idea or message through one or more language domains; listening, speaking, reading, or writing. It generally entails three criteria:

1. Comprehension and use of the specialized or technical vocabulary and language patterns associated with content

2. Linguistic complexity (length and variety of sentences and discourse), register (formality), organization, and cohesion of oral interaction or writing

3. Demonstration of understanding or usage of the sound system (phonology), the grammatical structure (syntax), and the meaning (semantics) of the language (Gottlieb, 2004b)

In contrast, academic achievement focuses on the skills and knowledge that underlie the communication. Academic language proficiency in the area of social studies might be exemplified by the use of the grammatical pattern: "The president

Figure 2.1 The Relationship Among Social Language Proficiency, Academic Language Proficiency, and Academic Achievement

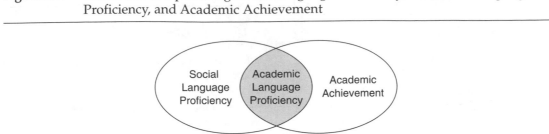

SOURCE: Gottlieb (2003).

of the United States is . . . The governor of California is . . . The mayor of Los Angeles is . . ."; for academic achievement, however, the students would be expected to supply each of those facts correctly. Figure 2.1 illustrates how the construct of academic language proficiency emerges at the intersection of social language proficiency and academic achievement.

The reflection in Appendix 2.1 applies the principles of language proficiency and academic achievement to classroom practice. In it, there are some ideas for targets of language proficiency and academic achievement that could be incorporated into the same content-based lesson. This dual focus on language and content in lesson planning can then be reflected in teachers' instruction and assessment of English language learners.

THE SECOND LANGUAGE ACQUISITION PROCESS

All English language learners acquire a second language following a series of predictable, developmental stages that form a continuum. This continuum is arbitrarily divided into levels, from little proficiency to that of being proficient in English. By knowing the language proficiency level of their second language learners, teachers can better plan instruction and assessment to meet the students' individual needs.

Generally, students' receptive language (listening and reading) is more advanced than their productive language (speaking and writing) at a given level (Gottlieb & Hamayan, 2002; Krashen & Terrell, 1983; Spolsky, 1989). That is, although English language learners may speak English quite fluently, they still may not have the academic language to communicate content through writing at the same level of proficiency. Figure 2.2 shows a sequence of five proficiency levels of second-language acquisition.

Figure 2.2 A Continuum Marking Second-Language Acquisition

Level 1   Level 2   Level 3   Level 4   Level 5

Lowest level of language proficiency • Highest

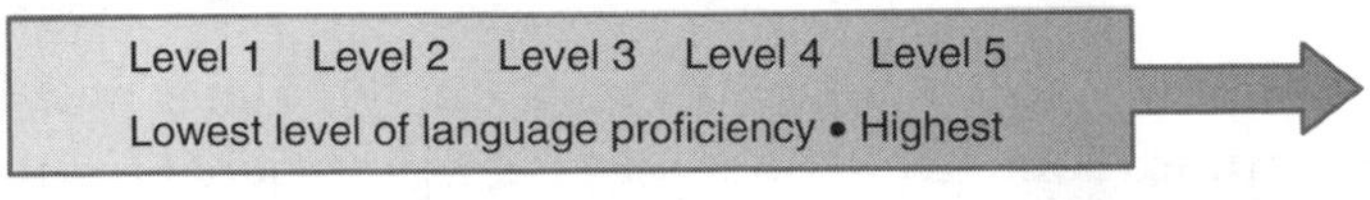

Although all English language learners acquire a second language by passing through the series of levels, their pace of acquisition varies. Students who are literate in their **native language**, with continuous schooling, will move through the levels more rapidly than those who do not have such a strong foundation or whose education has been limited or interrupted.

Students may also start along different points along the continuum. Some English language learners may have had previous exposure to English as a foreign language outside the United States and have gained some literacy skills. Within this country, some English language learners may have preschool experiences; others may have siblings or other family members who interact in two languages. Still others, typically at beginning levels of English language proficiency, have not been previously exposed to English, whether being newcomers or born here.

Levels of Language Proficiency

The second language acquisition continuum offers teachers a generalized scheme of the language English language learners comprehend and produce. Table 2.2 is a summary of the features of second language development across five language proficiency levels. The levels are summaries of English language learners' expectations for receptive and productive language. Their descriptors are useful for teachers to communicate to one another about a student's overall language development, group students, and plan differentiated instruction and assessment.

One of the salient features of second language acquisition is students' use of vocabulary. At the beginning levels of language proficiency, English language learners typically rely on high-frequency, common words, such as *animal*. As more language is acquired, general language emerges, such as *bear*. At the higher levels of language proficiency, students often use more technical, descriptive terms, such as *grizzly*.

REFLECTION: Grouping English Language Learners

Table 2.2 presents a thumbnail sketch of the criteria associated with each level of language proficiency. Using this information as a starting point, how would you group your English language learners according to their receptive and productive language? You may wish to complete the blank chart in Appendix 2.2 with the names of your students or additional criteria.

Types of Support for English Language Learners

English language learners at the early levels of language proficiency need linguistic (such as opportunities to interact with other language models), graphic (such as the use of tables or graphic organizers), or visual **supports** during instruction and assessment to assist them in accessing and constructing meaning. For visual support, real-life objects are the most authentic and tangible; however, any concrete referent

Table 2.2 The Salient Features of Second Language Development From the Lowest to Highest Level of Language Proficiency

At their given level of English language proficiency, English language learners will . . .		
	Comprehend (through listening and reading)	Produce (through speaking and writing)
Level 5	Technical vocabulary and language patterns of when presented with a variety of sentences of varying language complexity in extended discourse.	Cohesive, organized, and fluent language that includes technical vocabulary with developmental errors similar to those of proficient English peers.
Level 4	Specialized and some technical vocabulary and language patterns of content when presented with a variety of sentences of varying language complexity.	Organized language that includes specialized vocabulary with minimal errors that do not impede the overall meaning of the communication.
Level 3	General and some specialized vocabulary and language patterns of content when presented with a variety of expanded sentences with some support.	Language with hesitancy that includes general and some specialized vocabulary marked with errors that may impede the communication but retain much of the meaning.
Level 2	General, high-frequency language related to content when presented with short sentences that have visual or graphic support.	Halting language with high-frequency vocabulary marked with errors that tend to impede the meaning of the communication.
Level 1	Some language patterns (phrases and short sentences) when presented with visual and graphic support.	Pictorial and graphic representation of the language with sporadic words, phrases, and memorized chunks of language.

SOURCE: Adapted from Gottlieb (2004b).

is helpful. Table 2.3 provides examples of some types of supports for instruction and assessment available for these students.

Irrespective of English language learners' stage of English language development, with visual, graphic, and linguistic support these students can engage in higher-level thinking. For example, English language learners at the intermediate grade levels can compare and contrast characters, scientific objects, quantities, or historical time periods using a variety of graphic organizers. Older English language learners can construct scientific models, graphs, charts, or timelines based on data or information in lieu of writing lengthy essays or reports.

As English language learners accrue more language proficiency and move through the second language continuum, these supports are gradually reduced, in accordance with students' age and grade level. At the highest levels of language proficiency, students should be working with grade-level materials with some modifications.

Table 2.3   Types of Support for English Language Learners

Linguistic Support	Graphic Support	Visual Support
• Use of native language • Definition of key terms within sentences (e.g., "What are your plans this weekend; tell me what you are going to do on Saturday and Sunday.") • Modification of sentence patterns (i.e., avoiding passive voice) • Use of redundancy or rephrasing • Opportunities to interact with proficient English models	• Charts (i.e., pie, T) • Tables (i.e., histogram) • Timelines, number lines • Graphs • Graphic organizers (i.e., Venn diagrams, semantic webs)	• Real objects (i.e., maps, coins, rocks) • Manipulatives (i.e., cubes, Cuisenaire rods) • Photographs • Pictures, illustrations • Diagrams • Models (i.e., displays) • Magazines, newspapers • Videos • Multimedia, including Internet

Ideas for Assessing English Language Learners at Varying Language Proficiency Levels

Teachers who may not be familiar with second language methodologies or who have not worked with English language learners are often challenged when it comes to measuring language or content. The easiest classroom strategy to remember is that activities (and languages) used for instruction of English language learners can also serve for assessment. Table 2.4 lists suggestions for teachers to use with English language learners from English language proficiency Level 1, the lowest, to Level 5, the highest.

The final section of this chapter sheds further light on how to approach instruction and assessment of English language learners through standards. We see how English **language proficiency standards** are designed according to English language proficiency levels and how English language learners gain access to **academic content standards.**

LANGUAGE PROFICIENCY AND ACADEMIC CONTENT STANDARDS

Thus far, we have noted that language proficiency represents language in social and academic settings, whereas academic achievement is tied to knowledge and skills of specific content areas. English language learners' language proficiency pinpoints their place on the language acquisition continuum; their academic achievement reflects their overall conceptual development. This distinction also plays itself out in

Table 2.4 Instructional Assessment Ideas for English Language Learners at Varying Language Proficiency Levels

Level 5	• Justify and defend positions through speeches, multimedia reports, or essays • Research and investigate academic topics using multiple resources • Explain relationships, consequences, or cause and effect • Debate issues • React and reflect on articles, short stories, or essays of multiple genres from grade-level materials • Author poetry, fiction, nonfiction for varied audiences
Level 4	• Explain processes or procedures with extended discourse/paragraphs • Produce original models, demonstrations, or exhibitions • Summarize and draw conclusions from speech and text • Construct charts, graphs, and tables • Discuss pros and cons of issues • Use multiple learning strategies
Level 3	• Compare and contrast objects, people, events with sentences • Outline speech and text using graphic organizers • Use information from charts, graphs, or tables • Make predictions, hypotheses based on illustrated stories, events, or inquiry • Take notes • Produce short stories, poetry, or structured reports with support
Level 2	• Name and describe objects, people, or events with phrases • Plot timelines, number lines, or schedules • Follow multiple-step directions • Define and categorize objects, people, or events with visual or graphic support • Analyze and extract information in charts and graphs • Sequence pictures with phrases
Level 1	• Identify objects, illustrations, symbols, or words by pointing or naming • Match and label pictures and words • Follow one-step directions • Sort objects or illustrations with words into groups • Illustrate and label words in graphic organizers • Make collages or photojournals about stories or topics

two sets of standards for English language learners. Language proficiency standards are used as the basis for measuring students' progress and attainment of English language proficiency; state academic content standards are the anchor for measuring academic achievement.

Standards and English Language Learners

Since the late 1980s, national organizations, beginning with the National Council of Teachers of Mathematics (1989), have developed content standards to describe what students should know and should be able to do as the result of schooling. By the early 1990s, other professional organizations followed suit, including the National Council of Teachers of English (NCTE), the International Reading Association (IRA), the National Research Council (which produced the National Science Education Standards), and the National Center for History in the Schools (Gómez, 2000). The groundbreaking work of the past decade serves as the foundation for today's state academic content standards.

Standards have played a prominent role in federal legislation, in particular, the reauthorization of the Elementary and Secondary School Acts. State academic content standards were introduced in the Improving America's School Act of 1994, and English language proficiency standards were mandated under the No Child Left Behind Act of 2001. Come this century, English language learners have emerged as an important student group and their unique linguistic and cultural characteristics have been acknowledged. Table 2.5 compares the features of English language proficiency standards for English language learners with academic content standards for all students.

Table 2.5   A Comparison Between Language Proficiency Standards and Academic Content Standards, as Distinguished in the No Child Left Behind Act

English Language Proficiency Standards	*Academic Content Standards*
• Designed for English language learners	• Designed for all students
• Centered on acquiring social and academic language proficiency	• Centered on achieving academically
• Organized by grade-level cluster, K–12 (such as K–2, 3–5, 6–8, and 9–12)	• Organized by grade level, from 3–8 and one grade level in high school
• Represented by four language domains: listening, speaking, reading, and writing	• Represented by the content areas of English language arts/reading, mathematics, and science
• Labeled according to levels of language proficiency (such as beginning, developing, transitioning)	• Labeled according to levels of achievement (such as basic, proficient, or advanced)
• Aligned with curriculum, instruction, and English language proficiency assessment	• Aligned with curriculum, instruction, and assessment of academic achievement

Building a pathway between language proficiency and academic achievement maximizes access of our English language learners to enhanced learning opportunities. The creation and implementation of rigorous and comprehensive English language proficiency standards facilitate this journey. By systematically defining the language of schooling associated with social and academic development in language

Figure 2.3   Bridging English Language Proficiency and Academic Content Standards Through Concepts

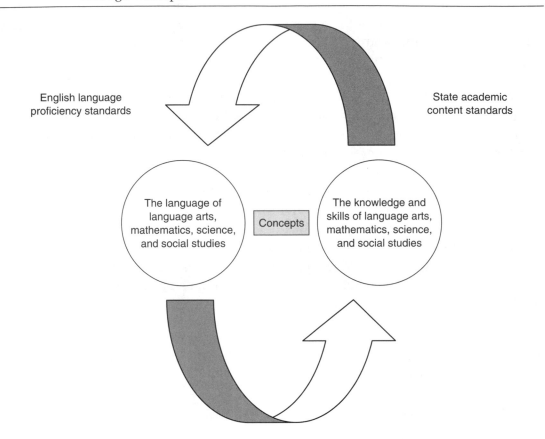

proficiency standards, English language learners, with sound instruction, can more readily learn the knowledge and skills of state academic content standards. Figure 2.3 illustrates how concepts bridge English language proficiency and academic achievement for English language learners.

National and State English Language Proficiency Standards

The federal government has played a sizeable role in the standards movement. Since 2003, all states have been required to develop and use English language proficiency standards grounded in their academic content standards. Appendix 2.3 provides a **checklist** to help teachers and administrators analyze their state's or district's English language proficiency standards in light of federal regulations.

Teachers of English to Speakers of Other Languages (TESOL), an international association of English language educators, has been prominent in the national scene for its contributions to standards-based education. Its *PreK–12 ESL Standards* (TESOL, 1997) has served as a template for state and school district adoption or adaptation across the country. The organization is planning to publish an updated, revised version based on the work of a multi-state consortium (State of Wisconsin, 2004). Its revised English language proficiency standards are listed in the following box.

The TESOL English Language Proficiency Standards (2006)

Standard 1: English language learners communicate for social, intercultural, and instructional purposes within the school setting.

Standard 2: English language learners communicate information, ideas, and concepts necessary for academic success in the area of language arts.

Standard 3: English language learners communicate information, ideas, and concepts necessary for academic success in the area of mathematics.

Standard 4: English language learners communicate information, ideas, and concepts necessary for academic success in the area of science.

Standard 5: English language learners communicate information, ideas, and concepts necessary for academic success in the area of social studies.

Language Proficiency Standards and Second Language Development

Language proficiency standards reflect how language is developed through content for second-language learners across the language domains of listening, speaking, reading, and writing. Within the standards, language proficiency levels (such as in Table 2.2) describe how students use language through a series of progress or performance indicators, measurable indices of students' language behaviors. By sharing this information, teachers gain an understanding of the progressive levels of language proficiency as the starting point for collaboration and joint planning.

Progress or Performance Indicators

Progress or performance indicators, the core and most discrete component of English language proficiency standards, are composed of multiple elements:

- The language function carries the communicative intent or action; it identifies how the students use language.
- The **content stem** provides the context or content in which the intent or action is embedded.
- The support offers visual or graphic avenues, when combined with language, to enhance comprehension (Gottlieb, 2004b).

For example, in the performance indicator for a language proficiency standard that addresses the language of science, "**Describe** scientific events or discoveries based on illustrations or photographs," the word *describe* is the language function, "scientific events or discoveries" is the content stem, and "illustrations or photographs" is the form of visual support.

As English language learners progress through the levels of English language proficiency, language patterns become more complex (e.g., from single words or phrases to simple, short sentences in the present tense to extended sentences with embedded clauses) while the quantity, quality, and control of language increase. In the example that follows, the language functions are bolded to illustrate how, within **a strand** of performance indicators related to science for middle-grade students, English language learners move from labeling concrete objects to defending the results of science inquiry.

English Language Proficiency Standards: A Sample Strand of Performance Indicators in the Area of Science for Middle-Grade English Language Learners

Level 5: **Explain and justify** why hypotheses prove true or false based on the results of experiments (e.g., "My hypothesis is (not) true because _____").

Level 4: **Describe** possible results of experiments based on hypotheses (e.g., "If I _____, then _____).

Level 3: **Outline** the steps involved in inquiry based on scientific hypotheses (e.g., "First, I need to . . . Second, . . . Third, . . . Last, . . .") using a graphic organizer.

Level 2: **Produce** scientific hypotheses using phrases or illustrations (e.g., "I think that _____") from model sentences.

Level 1: **Record and label** scientific objects, materials, and equipment for conducting scientific inquiry (e.g., "This is a _____").

Differentiating Instruction and Assessment by Levels of English Language Proficiency

English language proficiency standards, by describing progressive and scaffolded levels of language development, provide a natural venue for generating ideas on how to differentiate instruction and assessment for English language learners. Teachers' awareness of the levels of language proficiency, along with individual strands of performance indicators, help target lesson and unit planning. Although all students are engaged in scientific inquiry, for example, the expectations of English language learners should reflect their **level of language proficiency**. Table 2.6 takes the performance indicators from the above science strand and converts them into an assessment checklist by level of language proficiency.

English language proficiency standards are anchored in academic content standards. As such, teachers need to use both sets of standards for continuity of instruction and assessment. In the next section, we see how academic content standards work in conjunction with English language proficiency standards in teaching English language learners.

Academic Content Standards and Second Language Development

Ultimately, English language learners must attain proficiency in English and achieve academically. Introduction to content, however, needs to be in accordance

Table 2.6 An Assessment Checklist Based on a Strand of Performance Indicators in the Area of Science

English Language Proficiency Level	Expectations for English Language Learners
Level 5	• Connect cause and effect based on scientific inquiry • Give reasons for results of scientific inquiry based on evidence
Level 4	• Produce a short scientific report from questions • Answer scientific questions under varying conditions
Level 3	• Narrate steps of the inquiry • Outline steps to conducting scientific inquiry
Level 2	• Make statements to be verified or negated • Formulate questions
Level 1	• Match materials and scientific equipment with labels • Identify materials and scientific equipment (e.g., by pointing)

with the students' levels of English language proficiency. The pathway to state academic content standards, therefore, has to be carefully delineated so that English language learners can ultimately succeed in school.

The state of Wisconsin has created a system for teachers for helping English language learners reach academic goals. In it, performance indicators have been deconstructed from the academic content standards so that they are more readily attained by second language learners. The example that follows shows how performance indicators for an academic content standard for physical science have been adjusted, yet maintain their rigor, for English language learners.

Academic Content Standards: Sample Performance Indicators in the Area of Science for Fourth Grade (State of Wisconsin, 2002)

Performance indicator for proficient English students	Adjusted Performance Indicators for English language learners
Understand that substances can exist in different states	1. Identify examples of states of matter
	2. Label and sort items as solid, liquid, or gas

In addition, there are suggestions for assessment activities for English language learners that match the alternate performance indicators. Whereas proficient English speakers may be able to obtain and demonstrate their knowledge through text, English language learners show what they know through other means. For the sample performance indicators related to the "states of matter," English language learners, in science class, may do the following:

- Point to real-world examples or illustrations of solids, liquids, or gases
- Categorize real-world examples or illustrations according to states of matter
- Match real-world examples or illustrations with labels
- Observe and record changes in states of matter

To provide a continuous pathway for English language learners, the performance indicators for academic content standards need to align with those of English language proficiency. Taking the English language proficiency standards developed by a consortium in which Wisconsin is the lead state, the match becomes apparent. In Grades 3 through 5, for the language of science, the model performance indicators for English language proficiency (for listening) state that English language learners, at Level 1, "identify examples of physical states of matter . . . from oral statements with visual support," and Level 2, "distinguish among examples of physical states of matter . . . from oral statements and visual support" (State of Wisconsin, 2004). Thus we see how English language proficiency standards work in tandem with those for academic content standards for second language learners.

Standards-Based Assessment

In today's classroom, standards are the cornerstone for accountability. Content standards are the starting point, anchor, and reference for teaching and learning. English language proficiency standards lead to instruction and assessment of English language proficiency, and academic content standards are geared to instruction and assessment of academic achievement.

English language proficiency standards do not exist and function in isolation; they complement academic content standards. Teachers often combine multiple standards, as well as their performance indicators, to create thematic units of study. Thematic instruction that centers on a guiding set of principles or "big ideas," where students are active participants, is advantageous for English language learners (Enright & McCloskey, 1988; Freeman & Freeman, 2000; Manning, Manning, & Long, 1994). Through differentiated, **content-based instruction**, teachers can cover standards more comprehensively and assess English language learners in more appropriate ways.

SUMMARY AND FINAL THOUGHTS

English language proficiency and academic achievement are partners in the education of English language learners. Teachers who are aware of their students' social and academic language proficiency in English and their academic achievement in English or their native language are better prepared to provide a systematic, continuous, and appropriate, content-grounded education.

In recent years, there has been an increased commitment to the education of English language learners. As English language learners are recognized contributors to each state's accountability system, educators have become sensitive to the need to shift from social language proficiency to academic language proficiency as the basis for curriculum, instruction, and assessment.

The value of having English language proficiency standards for English language learners is undeniable. For the first time in the more than forty years of federally supported services, states must formally recognize this unique student population by describing second language development through a series of language proficiency levels. English language proficiency standards benefit English language learners and their teachers by providing groundwork for the following:

- Grade-level cluster curriculum, minimally in language arts/reading, math, and science
- Differentiated instruction through the use of sheltered techniques or native language support in the content areas for the varying English language proficiency levels
- A coordinated set of instructional services and assessment measures

In bridging language proficiency to academic achievement, we are able to provide enhanced educational opportunities, practices, and academic challenges for second-language learners. We have created the stepping-stones for English language learners to reach academic parity with their proficient English-speaking peers. Most important, we have energized the educational community to act on behalf of our students.

APPENDIX 2.1

REFLECTION: Purposes for Classroom Assessment, Types of Measures, and Language of Assessment

In this table, there is a list of possible types of measures associated with a purpose for classroom assessment of English language learners (those that do not fit are marked with an X). Based on your personal knowledge, or that of other teachers in your school, write the names of the measures that are used in the designated box. Then discuss with other teachers how you use the information obtained from assessment.

Language Proficiency Target	*Academic Achievement Target*
Compare size of objects using superlatives	Measure objects with a ruler
Describe what you might see in a capital city	Name and locate state capitals
Use sequential language to identify points on a timeline	Produce a timeline according to dates of events
Give examples of where to find letters of the alphabet	Recite the alphabet
Select furniture for a room based on perimeter and justify choices	Find the perimeter of a room
Discuss why oxygen is important to our lives	Classify chemical compounds by presence or absence of oxygen

APPENDIX 2.2

*Grouping English Language Learners
by Levels of Language Proficiency*

At their given level of English language proficiency, English language learners will . . .		
	Comprehend (through listening and reading)	Produce (through speaking and writing)
Level 5		
Level 4		
Level 3		
Level 2		
Level 1		

APPENDIX 2.3

A Checklist for Evaluating English Language Proficiency Standards

Do your state's or district's English language proficiency standards have the following features? Put an X under YES or NO to indicate whether the standards have the following criteria:

Are your state or school district's English language proficiency standards . . .	YES	NO
Observable, measurable, and clearly stated		
Cognitively engaging for students across the levels of language proficiency		
Reflective of both social and academic language required of schooling		
Representative of the developmental continuum of second language acquisition		
Supported visually or graphically		
Descriptive of defined levels of English language proficiency		
Aligned across grade-level clusters (vertically)		
Aligned across language proficiency levels (horizontally)		
Balanced in terms of the degree of specificity of performance or progress indicators		
Balanced in coverage of the language domains: listening, speaking, reading, and writing		
Anchored in state academic content standards—minimally, language arts/reading, mathematics, and science		
Illustrative of a seamless transition from English language proficiency to academic content standards (horizontally aligned)		
Ecologically valid—that is, do the standards help inform curriculum and instruction		
Amenable to large-scale state, district, and classroom assessment		
Directly tied to the state's English language proficiency assessment		

3

Assessing Oral Language and Literacy Development

The Bridge From Social Language Proficiency to Academic Language Proficiency

There is a land of the living and a land of the dead, and the bridge is love.

—Thornton Wilder, *The Bridge of San Luis Rey*

Assessments for English language learners generally have not been able to predict students' readiness for full participation in mainstream classrooms (Bailey & Butler, 2002; Cummins, 1981), yet certain instructional strategies have proven effectiveness in promoting language development (Genesee, 1987; Mohan, 1986; Short, 1993; Snow & Brinton, 1997). Our assessments must match best instructional practice, reflect the characteristics of English language learners, and yield useful information. For our students to reap educational benefits, teachers must contribute to the conversation on what constitutes fair assessment for English language learners.

This chapter proposes ideas for assessing English language learners' **language proficiency** (oral language and literacy development). It does so from two vantage points—that is, from both large-scale and classroom perspectives. In this way, teachers can become familiar with the techniques used to obtain evidence of student performance.

Each section highlights a **language domain** and suggests activities and tasks associated with language proficiency assessment. Listening, speaking, reading, and writing are presented separately because they are treated independently in English **language proficiency standards** and state assessment. In this way, teachers will be able to design a profile of English language learners' receptive and productive language.

LANGUAGE PROFICIENCY ASSESSMENT: ORAL LANGUAGE

For English language learners, oral language development most likely proceeds in two languages. Even though enrolled in school, second language learners will continue to be exposed to their first, or native, language at home and in settings frequented by family members. Reinforcement of students' first language in school either informally, through peer interaction, or through formal instruction is a school district or state policy. Notwithstanding, it remains the responsibility of teachers to capitalize on the linguistic and cultural resources of their students by making connections with their prior experiences.

English language learners should be encouraged to use their first language, especially at the onset of **second language acquisition**, and the extent that the first language is an instructional aid or tool should be reflected in **classroom assessment** practices. Younger students might seek assistance from paraprofessionals, other adults, or even peers. Older students, if literate, might consult a bilingual dictionary or have access to their **native language** through the Internet. Whichever resources are afforded English language learners for instruction should automatically extend to assessment.

Listening and speaking naturally interact. Although maintaining real-life contexts of language acquisition is a mainstay of instruction, in some instances, teachers must be able to isolate the language domains during assessment. Listening comprehension is generally the first step in acquiring language. Knowing that English language learners most likely have greater comprehension than language production, it is advantageous for teachers to have a grasp of the extent to which their students understand oral language.

The Nature of Listening Comprehension

Listening in a second language entails the same auditory processing as for a first or native language. Both first and second language learners tend to make the same types of errors. However, the reasons behind the errors differ. English language learners may experience difficulty in listening comprehension in their second language due to the following:

1. Not being acclimated to the linguistic system

2. Unfamiliarity with the sociocultural context of the message

3. Differing background knowledge

4. The influence of their first language (Buck, 2001)

There are various purposes for assessing listening comprehension of English language learners. **Discrete-point** testing, in which the elements of language are isolated, may be appropriate for diagnosing specific linguistic aspects of listening. Phonemic discrimination tasks, such as recognizing minimal pairs (where the sole distinction between words is a sound or phoneme, as in *chip* and *ship*, *pat* and *pet*, *dear* and *deal*) are examples of this approach.

Communicative approaches, on the other hand, tend to emphasize the message or how language is used in a particular situation or context rather than knowledge of the language per se. The emphasis is on the broader communication, or listening comprehension, rather than on listening as a subskill (Madsen, 1983). In other words, listening comprehension as a component of language proficiency is an expression of communicative competence (Hymes, 1972). The overriding characteristic of communicative assessment is the use of real-world or authentic text or materials that portray realistic situations and prompt natural interaction. This approach has greatest applicability to the classrooms with English language learners (Cohen, 1994).

Classroom Assessment of Listening Comprehension

At the classroom level, teachers can promote the oral language development of their second language students through a variety of activities that stem from a standards-based curriculum. English language learners should always be instructed just above their current language proficiency level, as first stated in the input hypothesis (Krashen, 1992). However, assessment should be geared to what the students can verbally produce or demonstrate nonverbally.

Teachers are often the primary second language model for English language learners. Throughout the school day, additional sources of oral input may help promote second language students' listening comprehension, including cassette tapes, videos, and DVDs, as well as interaction with school personnel, adult volunteers, older students, and peers.

English language learners may demonstrate their listening comprehension in nonverbal ways. Those students at the beginning stages of second language acquisition may simply point to the key characters, places, or objects in an illustrated book in response to questions or commands. Younger students may listen to a story while viewing its illustrations and then role play or reenact key events. Older students might compare the traits of two characters from a teacher's oral reading by selecting words or phrases from a bank (read orally) and using them in a Venn diagram or another type of graphic organizer. Another option would have students classify a series of events that occur before and after a pivotal even.

English language learners must actively engage in learning and demonstrate what they have learned in hands-on ways. Table 3.1 lists several classroom examples of instructional assessment activities that center on listening comprehension. It is followed by Table 3.2, which converts these activities into an assessment **checklist** for use across the core content areas.

Documenting Listening Comprehension

Teachers must plan how to document listening comprehension of English language learners. There are several ways of tracking student progress at the classroom level: (1) anecdotal evidence, (2) checklists, or (3) standards-based **rubrics**. To collect anecdotal information, teachers can target individual English language learners throughout a week with a specific **strand** of performance indicators for listening from an English language proficiency standard. For example, Table 3.2 illustrates a listening strand on learning strategies across five levels of language proficiency aimed at the middle school level.

Teachers could copy or modify the strand of performance indicators and mark the language proficiency level of the students with the date, based on their overall performance on a series of tasks. Another approach to documenting listening comprehension would have teachers list the students, make reference to their language proficiency level, and add specific strategies used by individual students during a period of time.

By creating a checklist from the **language objectives** of a lesson or unit, teachers can tick whether their English language learners meet the language demands of instruction. Table 3.3 takes the different types of listening activities and converts them into a generic checklist for use across the core content areas.

Last, by designing rubrics from English language proficiency standards and levels of language proficiency, teachers can designate the language proficiency level that bests describes student performance at a given point in time, based on observed or concrete evidence. Used throughout the school year, all these assessment techniques yield rich information on the progress of English language learners in the area of listening comprehension.

Table 3.1   Sample Types of Performance Activities for Instructional Assessment of Listening Comprehension

Examples of Listening Activities for English Language Learners
• Constructing/filling in models, maps, timelines, or figures from oral directions • Identifying or locating symbols, icons, dates, numerals, places from models, maps, timelines, figures, or written text from oral statements • Sorting pictures or matching pictures/words/phrases based on oral descriptions • Reenacting or dramatizing narrative text read aloud • Sequencing illustrations or ordering diagrams based on oral discourse • Responding to oral commands or following oral directions • Drawing representations or completing graphic organizers, as directed orally • Designing charts, graphs, or tables based on oral input • Analyzing, interpreting, and evaluating information on charts, graphs, and tables, as directed orally

Table 3.2   A Sample Strand of Model Performance Indicators for Listening

Level 1	Level 2	Level 3	Level 4	Level 5
Match oral commands with learning strategies represented visually (e.g., "Write a word in the blank.")	Follow a set of oral directions involving learning strategies represented visually (e.g., "Look at the four answers. Choose the best one.")	Practice learning strategies with visual representation (e.g., "Let's answer the easy questions first.") from oral directions	Select and use learning strategies presented orally with familiar material	Apply multiple-learning strategies presented orally to new material

SOURCE: Adapted from State of Wisconsin (2004).

Large-Scale Assessment of Listening Comprehension

Listening is a language domain of English language proficiency standards that, in turn, serves as the anchor for English language proficiency **tests**. Unlike classroom assessment where teachers can readily rely on realia (real-life objects), **manipulatives**, or role play as vehicles for students' expression of listening comprehension, **large-scale assessment** generally must depend on line art, photographs, or other forms of graphics or visual support. Assessment of listening comprehension in the classroom often relies on the interaction between a teacher and an individual student in a natural setting. In contrast, large-scale assessment of listening comprehension is generally confined to a paper-and-pencil test administered to a sizeable group of students at one time.

Listening comprehension on large-scale assessment can involve various cognitive processes. English language learners can match speech with its visual representation, sequence pictures from an oral story, follow a series of oral directions to complete patterns, or categorize content-related objects described orally. Students can compare and contrast features present in illustrations, arrange icons or information on maps or timelines, or draw conclusions from cartoons. The same high levels of cognitive engagement can also be demonstrated through assessment of speaking, our next language domain.

The Nature of Speaking

Speaking generally involves two-way communication with interactive role switching between the speaker, who conveys a message, and the listener, who interprets and responds to it (Underhill, 1987). The negotiation of meaning between two or more persons is always related to the context in which it occurs (O'Malley & Pierce, 1996). Based on this perspective, oral language is viewed as a purposeful, communicative action with emphasis on the specific use (the **language function**) or performance.

Table 3.3   An Assessment Checklist for Listening Comprehension

Check "Yes" or "No" or write the date in the appropriate box. You may also choose to write the name of the unit of instruction or provide more specific information on the type of activity.

Based on oral input, the English language learner can do the following:	Language Arts		Math		Science		Social Studies	
	Yes	No	Yes	No	Yes	No	Yes	No
Construct or fill in models, maps, timelines, and figures								
Identify or locate symbols, icons, dates, numerals, places, words, or phrases (from models, maps, timelines, figures, or text)								
Sort pictures or match pictures/ words/phrases								
Reenact or dramatize scenes or issues								
Sequence illustrations or order diagrams (such as cycles or processes)								
Respond to oral commands or follow directions								
Draw in response to oral directions; complete graphic organizers								
Design charts, graphs, tables, or other representations								
Analyze, interpret, and evaluate information on charts, graphs, and tables								

Speech can be deconstructed into discrete elements. The principal components of speech include grammar (or syntax), vocabulary (or the lexicon), intonation and stress, pronunciation, fluency, and accuracy (appropriateness of expression or register). Based on this perspective, oral language is envisioned as a linguistic system with emphasis on the code to be mastered (Baker, 1989).

Thus there are different ways of describing what it means to "know" or be "proficient" in a language—in this case, in reference to speaking. However, both have their place in the language classroom. Although the instructional assessment activities of the next section tend to focus on the communicative or message-bearing nature of language, teachers may choose to embed or highlight one or more components of speech within them.

Classroom Assessment of Speaking

Listening and speaking of English language learners go hand in hand. It is essential that second language learners, irrespective of their level of English language proficiency, have ample opportunities for speaking. Typical speaking activities that occur in classrooms as part of instructional assessment are found in Table 3.4.

As with all language teaching, differentiated approaches by language proficiency levels allow heterogeneous groups of English language learners to benefit from instruction. For students at the beginning of the second language acquisition continuum, a two-way task may be an appropriate **activity**. In it, each of paired English language learners has half the information on a graphic, such as location of places or landmarks on a map, and through commands or phrases, attempts to complete the missing half with the partner. More proficient students can engage in a similar activity but would be expected to use probing and questioning techniques to accomplish the same end.

Task analyses are another type of instructional assessment activity for relative newcomers to English that involves the use of sequential language in a series of descriptions. Descriptive task analyses or demonstrations can revolve around social language, such as how to tie a shoelace or how to play your favorite video or board game, or focus on academic language of the content areas, such as how plants grow from seeds or how cells undergo mitosis.

Certain language patterns accompany think-aloud activities. In assessing oral language proficiency, teachers should listen for phrases that denote how English language learners are processing and conveying the information rather than relating

Table 3.4   Sample Types of Activities for Instructional Assessment of Speaking

Examples of Speaking Activities for English Language Learners
• Book talks in which story grammar (characters, setting, events) is revealed
• Debates on school-related topics or current issues
• Dialogues between students on social or culturally related topics
• Interviews between students or between students and adults
• Presentations/reports on content-related assignments
• Role plays/dramatizations of historical or social events
• Speeches or reports based on research or topics of interest
• Task analyses or demonstrations on how to do activities, processes, or procedures
• Story (re)telling from illustrations or personal experiences
• Student-led conferences on original work or portfolios
• Think-alouds (personal reactions to reading) on articles, stories, or literature
• Two-way tasks on maps or missing information

specific facts related to the content. Phrases students may use to reflect their language proficiency include the following:

- I see . . .
- The title tells me that . . .
- The pictures help me . . .
- I think that the story is about . . .
- From what I read, I can predict that . . .
- The story reminds me of . . . .

Teachers need to explicitly instruct English language learners how to express themselves in a variety of ways. Keeping in mind students' level of oral language proficiency, those who are least proficient will rely on the most concrete referents and will use the more simple phrases, such as "I see." As English language learners acquire more language, they can begin to build complex sentence structures and become less reliant on visual or graphic support.

Documenting Classroom Assessment of Speaking

Documenting English language learners' oral production may be through direct observation or recording of speaking events. Data from teacher or district-level checklists or **rating scales**, derived from English language proficiency standards, offer evidence that English language learners are progressing in their second language. Table 3.5 shows a strand of performance indicators for speaking for an English language proficiency standard involving social and instructional language at the middle grades. Using this developmental scale as a documentation tool, teachers can mark the language proficiency level of their English language learners throughout the academic year based on classroom instruction.

Table 3.5 A Sample Strand of Model Performance Indicators for Speaking

Level 1	Level 2	Level 3	Level 4	Level 5
Repeat or give one word responses to questions or instructions	Retell or paraphrase instructions using phrases and short sentences	Summarize instructions using a series of sentences	Analyze and apply instructions using details in complex sentences	Explain instructions, appropriate for grade level, using extended discourse

SOURCE: Adapted from State of Wisconsin (2004).

Large-Scale Assessment of Speaking

Assessment of speaking involves a one-to-one interaction between an examiner (a teacher, diagnostician, or school psychologist) and an examinee (a student).

The major challenge of any large-scale attempt of speaking assessment is obtaining reliable information within a reasonable amount of time. Obviously, the larger the English language learner population in a school or school district, the logistics of collecting data becomes involved.

Several strategies can be employed, however, to overcome the obstacle of time for assessment. Because the quantity and quality of speech is a function of students' level of English language proficiency, students new to the country who have not been previously exposed to English cannot be expected to produce the same amount of discourse as students having received support services over an extended amount of time. Therefore, the speaking portion of an assessment should be adaptive to reflect a student's anticipated range of production. In addition, it may be more efficient to use an interview format with interrelated activities rather than ask a series of isolated questions.

In scoring speaking on a large-scale basis, teachers need to become familiar with the rubric or scoring guide used with the state's English language proficiency test. If, for example, speaking is to be assessed on the students' fluency, grammar, vocabulary, and comprehension, as in Table 3.6, teachers should direct instruction and classroom assessment incorporating those components.

Measuring oral language development of English language learners is only half the equation. The assessment of second language literacy is critical, especially with older students, because it is bound to academic success. The next sections examine aspects of reading and writing along with suggestions for assessment.

LANGUAGE PROFICIENCY ASSESSMENT: LITERACY

As with oral language development, literacy is often viewed along a developmental continuum (Hill, 2001; Tinajero & Ada, 1993) where placement denotes the position of students in relation to their ultimate proficiency. English language learners pass through a series of predictable stages as they acquire second language literacy; their pace is determined by their oral language proficiency in English, their literacy experiences in their native language, and their exposure to direct literacy instruction. Literacy development of English language learners deserves special attention because it is the cornerstone of academic success.

The Nature of Reading

Reading is a complex, multifaceted process. Reading comprehension is a mutually agreed-upon goal of the educational community; however, the pathway to its achievement has been hotly debated over the years. On this road to becoming a successful reader, there appears substantial evidence of a connection between reading comprehension and vocabulary development (Bauman, Kame'enui, & Ash, 2002; Nation, 2001; National Reading Panel, 2000). Other research-based components of reading English as a first language, starting with the Commission on Reading in 1985 with its release of *Becoming a Nation of Readers,* include early phonics instruction and use of reading strategies as key components of literacy instruction.

Table 3.6 An Example of a Speaking Rubric With Five Levels of Language Proficiency for Classroom and Large-Scale Use

	Language Proficiency Level				
Component	Level 1	Level 2	Level 3	Level 4	Level 5
Fluency	Fragmentary speech	Hesitant, telegraphic speech with long lapses	Conversant speech interrupted with some search for words and expressions	Generally fluent with strategies to compensate for challenging vocabulary or grammar	Fluid, flowing, effortless speech
Grammar	No evidence of syntactic structure	Consistent errors in word order and gaps in syntax impede communication	Frequent errors in word order at times obscure communication	Occasional errors in word order do not obscure communication	Word order approximates proficient English peers
Vocabulary	Isolated words and memorized expressions	High-frequency words and phrases	Use of social language with some academic words	Use of idioms and general academic language	Use of nuances and specific academic language similar to proficient English peers
Comprehension	Not readily apparent	Some understanding of social language when slow, repeated, or visually supported	General understanding of social language and some academic language in context	Complete understanding of social language and most academic language	Approaching full understanding of academic language of the content areas

Undeniably, recent research confirms that first or native language (**L1**) literacy influences second language reading development. Students who have a strong L1 literacy foundation acquire English literacy at a faster pace and reach parity with their native English peers sooner than those without the prerequisite skills (Christian & Genesee, 2001; Cummins, 1981; Slavin & Cheung, 2003, 2004). In other words, students' literacy in L1 is a stable predictor of their **L2** literacy (Pardo & Tinajero, 1993). This confirmatory evidence of the relationship between L1 and L2 literacy development is voiced by major national organizations that endorse L1 literacy instruction for English language learners (International Reading Association, 2001; International Reading Association & National Association for the Education of Young Children, 1998; Teachers of English to Speakers of Other Languages, 2001b).

Classroom Assessment of Reading

In a classroom setting, assessment of reading on a daily or **formative** basis often is coupled with either of the productive domains—speaking or writing. However, for comprehension purposes, there are certain times, such at the end of a grading period, when teachers should minimize the influence of other language domains to obtain a more accurate picture of a student's understanding of text in isolation. The approaches presented in Table 3.7 are associated with reading fluency, accuracy, and comprehension. All may readily be infused into an instructional routine that includes prereading, during-reading, and postreading strategies (Pierce, 2001) or that involves preview, view, and review (Freeman & Freeman, 2000) of literacy material.

A variety of instructional approaches, such as teacher modeled, shared, shared-to-guided, and guided reading, if employed systematically, results in students' gradually gaining independence as they acquire confidence and comprehension in reading. During shared reading, whole-group activities center on enlarged print materials, such as big books, charts, or word walls; English language learners beginning to read respond by pointing, highlighting or underlining, classifying or categorizing words or word families. Teachers frequently pause to check for comprehension or engage students in group discussion to brainstorm ideas.

Shared-to-guided reading is an instructional assessment technique developed for small groups of English language learners (*On Our Way to English,* 2004) that bridges these two approaches, providing teacher support as beginning readers describe

Table 3.7 Sample Types of Approaches for Instructional Assessment of Reading for English Language Learners

- Exploration of concepts about print
- Literature circles or book clubs
- Reciprocal or demonstration teaching
- Round-robin reading
- Shared reading
- Shared-to-guided reading
- Guided reading

illustrations, make predictions, and then track print and echo read. In guided reading, students read the text leveled specifically for English language learners independently, often in flexible small groups under the teacher's direction, while reading strategies are introduced. Teachers build on their students' strengths and stretch English language learners to new understandings through probing questions: For example, "What does the table of contents tell you?" "What clues do you have that this book is fiction or nonfiction?" "Did you find any surprises when you read the information?"

Documenting Classroom Assessment of Reading

Structured observation, where teachers systematically maintain written anecdotal records of their students, based on a preselected objective or standard, is a powerful classroom assessment tool (Shearer & Homan, 1994). Coupled with commercial or teacher-made checklists (Rhodes & Shanklin, 1993), teachers can focus on specific aspects of their students' literacy development and systematically document their performance over time.

REFLECTION: Documenting Literacy Development of English Language Learners Through Language Proficiency Standards

Look at the strands of model performance indicators in the listening and speaking sections. How might you convert either one of those to reading? How might the strand be used to help monitor students' progress? Share with another teacher your ideas for documenting reading comprehension of English language learners at different levels of language proficiency.

With increased literacy development and the ability of students to balance the use of the graphophonic (sound/symbol relationship), syntactic (grammatical structure), and semantic (meaning) cues (Freeman & Freeman, 2000) come greater efficiency and accuracy in making meaning from print. As English language learners advance in comprehending text, they may engage in more sophisticated activities, such as participating in literature circles or book clubs. For English language learners, assessment, as instruction, is always presented in context and moves from a skills orientation to comprehension base. Examples of ideas of how to assess reading comprehension of English language learners are listed in Table 3.8.

For English language learners who can decipher print meaningfully without visual or graphic support, teachers can easily convert text into cloze exercises (where words from a reading selection are systematically deleted) for students to ascertain their reading comprehension in context. Consider a unit on safety where the language objective centers on the use of prepositions. In a rationale cloze, specific classes of words are targeted; in this instance, common prepositions are deleted within the text and replaced by blanks. A word bank above or below the passage, as shown in the box, allows English language learners to access the missing words more readily. Keeping the first and last sentences intact, the first blank should always be used as a practice question for students who are not familiar with the format.

Table 3.8   Ways for English Language Learners to Demonstrate Reading Comprehension

- Categorizing, classifying, or sorting icons, words, or phrases into groups (using illustrations or graphic organizers)
- Drawing based on written text
- Matching words with pictures, words, phrases, sentences; matching sentences with paragraphs
- Underlining or highlighting main ideas or supporting details
- Completing cloze exercises using a word bank (see example in text)
- Sequencing pictures, sentences, or paragraphs
- Responding to oral comprehension questions, such as in running records or written text supported visually

An Example of a Rationale Cloze Passage With a Word Bank Used to Assess the Use of Prepositions

A Problem in My Neighborhood

There is a problem in my neighborhood. Children have no safe place to run and play. The streets are filled 1. _____ cars and buses. There are many holes and cracks 2. _____ the sidewalk. There is garbage 3. _____ the ground.

The neighbors want to find a safe place 4. _____ children to play. They meet to talk 5. _____ the problem. They decide to build a playground. It will make the neighborhood a safe place for children 6. _____ play. Won't that be nice?

Word Bank					
about	on	for	in	to	with

At times, teachers may wish to rely on a holistic rubric to describe where English language learners fall on a reading comprehension scale. Based on evidence accrued over time, teachers can use students' level of English language proficiency as a means of communicating English language learners' overall reading development. Table 3.9 provides a generalized scheme of reading acquisition using a five-point scale for classroom teachers.

Large-Scale Assessment of Reading

For English language learners, reading comprehension is a function of both graphic and textual support; that is, students' understanding of text or print is facilitated through illustrations, photographs, tables, charts, and line art. Students' comprehension is also aided by bold print (to reinforce important points), a glossary (as a footnote to text), or the use of a bilingual or picture dictionary (to clarify meaning). These support mechanisms are considerations for large-scale assessment of reading for second language learners.

Table 3.9   Rubric of the Stages of Reading Development

L1	L2	Levels of Reading Proficiency
		Level 5: Competent Reader Comprehends explicit text, including content-related material. Begins to draw inferences from text with teacher guidance. Uses multiple strategies appropriately and consistently.
		Level 4: Expanding Reader Constructs meaning from most explicit text independently. Connects some academic content to personal experiences. Makes predictions and connections of familiar content to real-life situations with teacher guidance. Uses a growing number of strategies to gain meaning from print.
		Level 3: Developing Reader Comprehends familiar and predictable text that is often visually supported. Uses the sound/symbol correspondence to decipher unfamiliar words. Has developed a sight vocabulary of words in context. Begins to use strategies to gain meaning from print.
		Level 2: Emergent Reader Sometimes memorizes and repeats language patterns in books. Makes the connection between sounds, letters, words, and word families. Identifies some high-frequency words and phrases. Matches words and phrases to pictures.
		Level 1: Prereader Attends to pictures and diagrams in books but does not connect with words. Displays some concepts about print. Begins to recognize letters and sounds in context and identifies some environmental print.

SOURCE: Adapted from Gottlieb (1999a).

Most large-scale assessment of reading, especially at the state level, relies on multiple-choice responses. This format is not ideal for English language learners because students need additional time to process text and be able to decipher which choice is most relevant. As part of their language development, second language learners need to become familiar with the language of testing, the varied formats, and test-taking strategies.

Research suggests that in large-scale assessment, the use of some accommodation strategies, such as a glossary or extra time, tends to benefit all students who are not good readers (Kiplinger, Haug, & Abedi, 2002). More investigation is necessary to shed light on the connections between native and second language reading comprehension, how English language learners acquire reading differently from their native English speaking peers, and which strategies best support reading development for second language learners.

Connecting Oral Language With Literacy

English language learners need extensive practice in their new language. Unlike their native English-speaking peers who have been exposed to and have interacted in English since birth, English language learners have not had the same amount of input or the opportunities to experiment in their second language. Therefore, as English language learners are developing oral language proficiency, teachers should simultaneously make connections to print.

The language experience approach is one teaching technique that involves all four language domains and offers tremendous flexibility in its implementation. It is useful for English language learners in bridging oral language to literacy, prior experiences to new ones, social to academic language, and one culture to another. This multistep process directly involves students in small groups or as a whole class, guided by the teacher, and consists of the following steps:

- Stimulating oral language development through discussion of personal and familiar issues, topics, or stories
- Dictating and recording students' self-generated language
- Practicing and reinforcing reading the printed version
- Modifying the text or producing a written response (Brisk & Harrington, 2000; Dixon & Nessel, 1983)

The reflection in Appendix 3.1 suggests some other classroom links between oral language and literacy development.

The Nature of Writing

As with reading, writing is a literacy process by which students use their prior experiences and knowledge of the world to apply a variety of strategies to, ultimately, make meaning (Peregoy & Boyle, 1993). As in reading, writing is an interactive process; in this case, it involves the writer, other writers, and written or oral text (Eskey & Grabe, 1988; Richard-Amato, 2003). As with oral language, attempting to divorce writing from reading creates an artificial division between two naturally interrelated language domains.

Classroom Assessment for Writing

As its productive counterpart of speaking, assessment of writing must tap students' direct performance as demonstrated through writing samples. Given the variability of English language learners' writing in their native language and English, writing should be a mainstay of the curriculum, with students being offered a range of writing genres within their language proficiency level. Table 3.10 lists various types of writing products eventually expected of all English language learners.

Teachers' awareness of their students' level of English language proficiency is essential for selecting appropriate writing assignments in school. Students at the beginning stages of English language acquisition may express their thoughts

Table 3.10 Sample Types of Products Associated With Instructional Assessment
of Writing

- Illustrated autobiographies/biographies
- Brochures on content-related topics or classroom newsletters
- Descriptions of places, people, objects, events
- Dialogues, poetry, prose
- Drawings or reactions to reading
- Editorials/critiques in response to reading, such as from newspapers
- Expository paragraphs and essays
- Interactive journal entries/content-related learning logs
- Labels for figures, diagrams, illustrations
- Letters for social or business purposes
- Lists within authentic contexts (such as equipment for scientific inquiry)
- Memos or e-mails
- Narrations (fictional or nonfiction)
- Note taking of lectures/outlining of text
- Position or research papers or multimedia presentations
- Structured reports (such as from science lab)
- Summaries of oral presentations, stories, or articles
- Survey questionnaires, test questions, or interview forms

through drawing, labeling objects, generating lists, or perhaps providing brief responses to e-mail messages or questions. As they move through the writing acquisition continuum, students may venture into various genres, such as describing, narrating, fantasizing, stating opinions, or defending positions. At this point, English language learners start to engage in extended, process writing. The most sophisticated, usually older, writers begin to produce pieces much like their proficient-English peers, including critiques, reports, and research papers. Writing portfolios are useful tools for maintaining and managing original student samples as well as for documenting English language learners' progress over time (Gottlieb, 1995).

English language learners' social writing often reflects their personal and cultural experiences. It provides insight for teachers who may not be familiar with the students' backgrounds. The following sample is a description of a special day in Poland from a fifth grader's journal entry.

In Poland 1st June is Children's Day. On this day all children are very happy because they got a lot of presents. On this day schools are close. On Children's Day places like Grade America are free for all children. Yesterday was 1st June and I get from my parents a nice game.

For classroom assessment, students' written work should be interpreted with a rubric or scoring guide. Teachers and administrators should bear in mind that the writing rubric for English language learners must clearly represent the characteristics of this student population and be descriptive of the second language writing acquisition process. Table 3.11 is a five-point holistic rubric that offers broad indicators of the developmental nature of writing for second language learners.

Table 3.11   Holistic Rubric of the Stages of Writing Development in English

L2	Levels of Writing Proficiency
	Level 5: Competent Writer Communicates in extended discourse, approaching that of proficient English peers. Message is clear, organized, and cohesive. Sporadic errors do not distract from the meaning. Mechanics and conventions are consistently present.
	Level 4: Expanding Writer Communicates in sentence and paragraph form using a variety of syntactic structures and lengths. Message is clear, although it may be occasionally blurred by inappropriate selection of words, phrases, or grammatical patterns. Mechanics and conventions are generally present. Often shows residual influence of native language, such as use of prepositions.
	Level 3: Developing Writer Communicates in sentences, often repeating a syntactic pattern. Message is present but not clear because it is disrupted by inappropriate selection of words, phrases, or grammatical patterns. Mechanics and conventions are inconsistent. Often shows some influence of native language, such as syntactic order.
	Level 2: Emergent Writer Communicates in phrases and short sentences, often repetitive. No discernible message because of multiple errors in grammar, word selection, and mechanics. May rely on native language to express ideas.
	Level 1: Prewriter Creates pictures and isolated letters, usually large case, in strings (young children). May reproduce or produce some recognizable words. Strong influence of native language (older children).

Large-Scale Assessment of Writing

State academic content standards for writing within English language arts tend to address multiple genres, including description, narration, explanation, exposition, and persuasion. Large-scale writing assessment of English language learners should differentiate writing prompts according to students' language proficiency levels. For example, beginning writers can respond to description by producing labels, lists, or phrases from illustrations or graphics. More mature writers can provide vivid, detailed description along with connections to their personal lives or situations.

Direct assessment of writing on a large-scale, language proficiency measure should replicate the types of writing required of English language learners in everyday **activities, tasks,** and **projects**. Some states have developed rubrics for interpreting student writing that can readily be modified for English language learners. For example, Illinois, from 1996 to 2003, administered a reading and writing test specifically designed for English language learners. In the state writing rubric, three components (focus, organization, and support/elaboration) served all students, one was adapted (from conventions to mechanics), and one was unique (language production) for second language learners. In this way, a clear path was established for English language learners that marked their transition into the **general education program**.

SUMMARY AND FINAL THOUGHTS

Federal law mandates that English language learners be assessed annually with a standards-based, statewide English language proficiency test of listening, speaking, reading, and writing. It is important for teachers to recognize the elements that compose such large-scale language proficiency measures. Appendix 3.2 offers a checklist for states and school districts for analyzing their language proficiency instruments. The results from both large-scale and classroom assessments should provide teachers with substantial information for determining the progress of their English language learners as they move toward the attainment of English language proficiency.

Historically, instruction and assessment of English language learners have focused on **social language proficiency** across the language domains and, at times, have dovetailed with the content area of English language arts. With current theory, practice, and legislation emphasizing the integration of content with language, teachers must convey the language associated with academic proficiency while infusing the social language that English language learners need to thrive in our English speaking world. The next chapter addresses the academic side, illustrating how to assess the language and content of mathematics, science, and social studies for second language learners.

APPENDIX 3.1

REFLECTION: *Connections Between Oral Language and Literacy*

There are numerous ways to extend oral language into literacy development for English language learners. The following pairs of oral language and literacy activities can be combined to create powerful connections. Think about how you can incorporate some of these ideas into instruction and assessment.

Oral Language	*Literacy Extension*
1. Book talks	Create PowerPoint presentations about authors, using multiple sources
2. Debates	Research a topic, take a stance, and defend it
3. Demonstrations	Explain how to use a product or describe a process using visuals or graphics
4. Dialogues	Compose or react to a conversation between two people
5. Presentations	Make an illustrated poster board outlining the major points
6. Dramatizations	Produce a script or short play in small groups
7. Story retellings or predicting the conclusion of narratives	Rewrite stories from different perspectives or change the endings of narrative text

APPENDIX 3.2

A Checklist for Analyzing Features of Large-Scale Language Proficiency Tests

Feature	*Present*	*Absent*	*NA /Comments*
Philosophy/Underlying Premise			
1. The purpose(s) of the test is clearly stated.			
2. The purpose matches the intent of the users.			
3. The test is theoretically based.			
4. The test is standards based.			
5. The test represents best practice.			
Psychometric Properties			
6. Content validity is evident.			
7. Face validity is evident.			
8. Construct validity is evident.			
9. Predictive validity is evident.			
10. A process for establishing interrater agreement is outlined.			
11. Interrater agreement of at least .85 is suggested for performance sections.			
Test Content and Format			
12. The test measures social and functional language within a school setting.			
13. The test measures academic language of the content areas.			
14. The test is developmentally appropriate at each grade-level cluster.			
15. The test contains minimal linguistic, cultural, and socioeconomic status (SES) bias.			
16. The language domains are amply represented.			
17. The range of language proficiency levels is amply covered.			
18. Illustrations or graphics are appropriate and support text.			
19. Illustrations or graphics are clear.			

Feature	Present	Absent	NA /Comments
20. The format is organized and appealing.			
21. The items within subsections progress logically.			
Administration, Scoring, and Reporting			
22. Directions for administration are clear and concise.			
23. There are adequate numbers of sample items.			
24. Total administration time appears reasonable.			
25. Scoring requires establishing interrater agreement for performance sections.			
26. Scoring rubrics have clear-cut criteria.			
27. Scoring rubrics have classroom applications.			
28. Subscale scores and the total score are easy to derive.			
29. Scores are easy to interpret.			
30. Scores are vertically equated across forms and grade levels.			
31. Results provide graphic, numerical, and descriptive information.			
32. Score reports include disaggregated data that are contextualized for each subgroup.			
33. Scores are meaningful at state, district, and school levels.			
34. Results are meaningful to administrators and help inform services for English language learners.			
35. Results are meaningful to teachers and help inform instruction.			
34. Results are understandable to family members and reports are available in multiple languages.			
35. The technical manual provides information on the test's reliability, validity, fairness as well as numbers, languages, and description of students in the norming or field test population.			

4

Assessing Academic Language Proficiency and Academic Achievement

The Bridge to Accountability

We build too many walls and not enough bridges.

—Sir Isaac Newton

Ultimately, accountability for learning rests on students' academic performance. For English language learners, English **language proficiency** is a vehicle toward reaching that goal. This chapter addresses the language and content specific to mathematics, science, and social studies that are requisite for **English language learners** to navigate and succeed in school. While not an exhaustive treatment, it attempts to sensitize teachers to the complexities involved in learning English as an additional language.

CONTENT-BASED INSTRUCTION AND ASSESSMENT

In language proficiency **assessment**, we focus on language, whereas content provides the context for communicating the message. In the assessment of **academic achievement**, the roles are reversed; the skills and knowledge associated with content take precedence and the language demands are adjusted according to the students' language proficiency levels. In either case, **content-based instruction** and assessment are a natural fit for teachers of English language learners, whether in **English as a second language**, **bilingual** or **dual-language**, or **general education** classrooms.

Academic content standards serve as guideposts for assessment of both language proficiency and academic achievement. These standards, which represent the targets for academic achievement, also serve as the endpoints for English **language proficiency standards**. Thus English language learners who travel along the pathway of English language development are able to access the language of the content areas in a systematic way. Ultimately, at the highest level of English language proficiency, students will seamlessly bridge into grade-level content.

Whereas academic content standards help shape English language proficiency assessment, they are the exclusive source and anchor for measures of academic achievement. Assessments of English language proficiency and academic achievement need to be aligned with academic content standards to yield valid results. Figure 4.1 shows how standards work side by side for English language learners and how this partnership is represented in assessment and instruction.

Our kindergarten through Grade 12 students face state assessment of English language proficiency on an annual basis while they must simultaneously participate in state assessment of academic achievement starting at Grade 3. For English

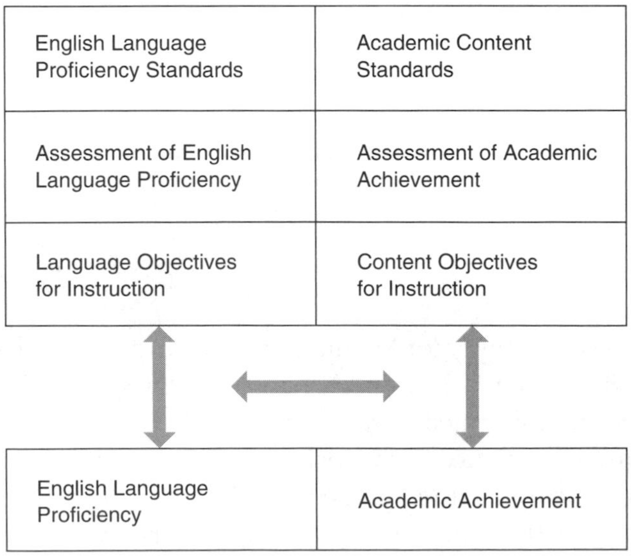

Figure 4.1   Alignment of Standards, Assessment, and Instruction of English Language Learners: The Bridge From Language Proficiency to Academic Achievement

language learners, acquiring the language of language arts, mathematics, science, and social studies (academic proficiency) has to correspond with learning the concepts and skills of the content areas (academic achievement). These high-stakes assessments, the foundation of statewide accountability systems, have influenced the instruction of English language learners.

The Nature of Content-Based Instruction

The shift in instructional practice for teachers serving English language learners has been gradual over the last decade. Much of language instruction at the elementary, secondary, and adult education levels has historically been drawn from the field of linguistics. Not until the 1980s and its merge with educational theory (Mohan, 1986) did we see students' language development coordinated with the content of subject matter. In the 1990s, we witnessed the debut of research-based instructional approaches that integrate language and content to foster academic growth of English language learners (Chamot & O'Malley, 1994). In 2000, a professional development model, grounded in research, further promoted sustained content-based instruction for English language learners (Echevarria, Vogt, & Short, 2000).

Large-scale assessment of English language learners, however, has not kept apace with the move to content-based instruction (Gottlieb, 2003). Although test publishers and consortia of states are developing large-scale measures of **academic language proficiency**, to this day, no measure of academic achievement has been specifically designed for this ever-growing student population. On the other hand, at the classroom level, teachers have responded to the need to prepare their students academically by incorporating content-based learning strategies into instruction and assessment practices for their English language learners.

ASSESSING LANGUAGE AND CONTENT

In planning instructional assessment, teachers working with English language learners have to consider both language and content. Appendix 4.1 lists features associated with language and content vertically and displays the core content areas horizontally. This matrix may be used at a classroom, school, or district level as a guide for designing assessment, mapping curriculum, and creating lessons for English language learners.

Every content area revolves around concepts marked by certain language patterns or discourse. English language learners who have mastered the concepts in their **native language** need only to attach the labels in English for known skills and knowledge that readily transfer from one language to the next. Other students will be challenged to simultaneously acquire language and content, a more lengthy process. The remaining sections of this chapter elaborate on the language and content of mathematics, science, and social studies and their associated assessment techniques.

The Language and Content of Mathematics

To begin the process of instructional assessment of English language learners, teachers must select appropriate targets. In introducing each content area, a **language**

objective, representative of a language proficiency standard, is presented side by side with a **content objective** from an academic content standard. In this way, teachers can visualize how language proficiency is distinct from, yet complements, academic achievement. These objectives are then transformed into ideas for instruction and assessment.

K–2 Language Proficiency Standard	K–2 Academic Content Standard
Language objective for assessment and instruction: *Use math terms when showing addition and subtraction of one-digit whole numbers with everyday objects*	Content objective for assessment and instruction: A*dd and subtract one-digit whole numbers*
Academic language proficiency	Academic achievement

It is a myth that mathematics is a universal language. For English language learners, operationally, mathematics is performed differently around the world (such as in the case of long division). Mathematical symbols may also differ (such as the use of the comma in some countries to designate the separation of whole numbers from their decimal parts). All students must learn the technical language or vocabulary specific to mathematics. However, in English, we tend to interchange numerous terms or expressions to signify one mathematical concept. These language patterns must be internalized by English language learners as equivalencies.

Various terms are used in English to trigger math calculation. Table 4.1 provides a list of key words associated with addition and subtraction. During instruction, teachers often interchange math sentences using varying grammatical structures with these key words and expressions. To illustrate this point, try this reflection.

REFLECTION: Defining Academic Language Proficiency

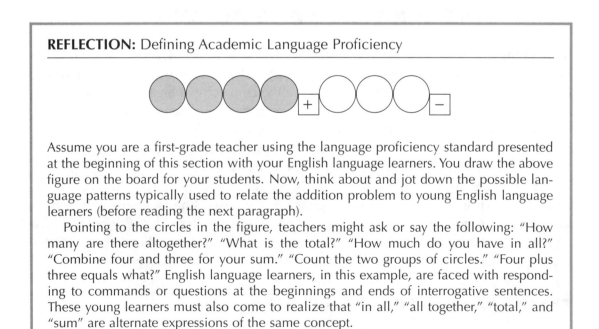

Assume you are a first-grade teacher using the language proficiency standard presented at the beginning of this section with your English language learners. You draw the above figure on the board for your students. Now, think about and jot down the possible language patterns typically used to relate the addition problem to young English language learners (before reading the next paragraph).

Pointing to the circles in the figure, teachers might ask or say the following: "How many are there altogether?" "What is the total?" "How much do you have in all?" "Combine four and three for your sum." "Count the two groups of circles." "Four plus three equals what?" English language learners, in this example, are faced with responding to commands or questions at the beginnings and ends of interrogative sentences. These young learners must also come to realize that "in all," "all together," "total," and "sum" are alternate expressions of the same concept.

Table 4.1   The Language of Math Operations

Addition	Subtraction
• And	• Take away
• Plus	• Take from
• More	• Minus
• More than	• Less (than)
• Altogether	• Diminished by (deduct)
• Increased by	• Are left
• Sum	• Remain
• In all	• Fewer
• Total	• Not as much as
• Combine	• Difference
• Add	• Subtract

Because English language learners have had limited practice in manipulating the syntax, or word order, of sentences, they cannot recognize how the same mathematical operation can be signaled in numerous ways (Crandall, 1987). Spanish speakers may recognize *sum* because the cognate carries to their native language (*suma*); however, *in all*, *altogether*, and *total*, all of which infer addition, are expressed only as *total* in Spanish. These words and expressions are not automatically acquired and internalized by students; teachers should introduce and reinforce each one independently.

As shown in the language of mathematical operations (a term in itself that carries multiple meanings), English language learners often struggle with mathematic terms that are high-frequency, everyday vocabulary. The word *table*, for example, is specific not only to mathematics (times table, data table) but has distinct meanings in social studies (table top or plateau), science (periodic table), language arts (table of contents, table the discussion), as well as being a common household object. Not only is the English language full of multiple meanings, it has nuances that are difficult for second-language learners to comprehend. When a teacher asks, "How many are left?" the reference is mathematical; with a subtle conversion to a prepositional phrase, "How many to the left?" the question now applies to directionality.

In English, word combinations often make mathematics conceptually compact, as in the phrase "least common denominator" or "two-thirds the base price." Even a phrase such as "percent off" where, in this instance, *off* means *reduction*, is confusing to English language learners who are more familiar with social language usage, as in "Turn *off* the light." Teachers must understand that for English language learners, acquiring the academic language proficiency involving the language of mathematics is as important as applying their mathematical knowledge for problem solving.

Classroom Instruction and Assessment

English language learners need to have concrete referents they can use to attach meaning to language and concepts. Besides linguistic, technological, visual, or graphic support, each content area has specific tools of its trade, so to speak. The following box displays some helpful math **supports** to be incorporated into instruction and assessment.

Manipulatives for Mathematics

- Clocks, sun dials, and other timekeepers
- Counters (including coins, abacus)
- Geometric figures
- Number lines
- Geoboards
- Rulers, yardsticks, nonmetric measures
- Compasses
- Calculators
- Protractors
- Scales, balances

To ascertain whether English language learners understand the language of mathematics, have them manipulate real objects such as unifix cubes, cuisenaire rods—whatever is developmentally appropriate, matches the objective of the lesson, and represents the performance indicator(s) of the language proficiency standard. Through a series of oral commands, teachers can observe whether students respond correctly, either nonverbally or orally. On the other hand, older students may listen to a teacher relate situations with embedded math problems. To demonstrate their comprehension of the language, the students may draw figures or construct graphs, charts, or tables.

Graphic representation lends itself to mathematical expression. The following problem uses a grid within a real-world context to help English language learners in middle school think mathematically and use math language in creative ways.

A Middle School Math Problem

Here are the floor plans for three different restaurants (A, B, and C). The shaded squares represent a bar; the other squares represent where people eat. You need to think about

- the fractional part or percentage of the restaurant that is the bar,
- the total area of the restaurant, and
- the difference in space between the bar and eating areas.

Decide which restaurant you would like to own. Explain, using math language, the reasons why you chose that one.

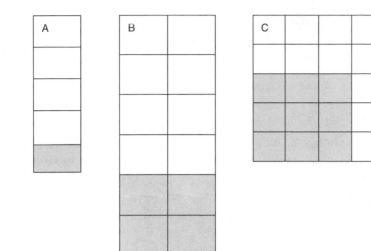

REFLECTION: Approaching Math for English Language Learners

After reading this math problem, you may wish to take a moment to answer the following questions:

What are its **language functions** (how are the students expected to use math language)?

What types of visual or graphic support, built into the problem, assist students in accessing meaning?

What would be a language objective (aimed at English language proficiency)?

What would be a content objective (aimed at academic content)?

How would you differentiate instruction and assessment for English language learners at various levels of English language proficiency?

English as a second language, bilingual, and general education teachers could collaborate to extend this problem into a multidisciplinary unit of study. In it, students could explore architecture (restaurant design), science (the effects of alcohol on your body), social studies (the pros and cons of having bars in restaurants), and English (creating ad campaigns for the restaurant, posters for the neighborhood, menus, or debating which of the restaurants would best serve their community). For assessment purposes, the students would need to know which language proficiency standards are addressed, the criteria used to interpret their work, how they are measured, and how each **activity** contributes to the final grade for the **project**.

In contrast with academic language proficiency, academic achievement in mathematics centers on the knowledge and skills required for problem solving. This underlying knowledge forms the basis for the manipulation of numbers to derive solutions to problems. Unlike for language proficiency, when addressing achievement, teachers ask whether students know their number facts, prove theorems, or apply the correct formulas. In the restaurant example above, students would have to determine fractions or percentages, calculate area, and subtract to arrive at their correct answers.

Large-Scale Assessment

In recent years, the distinction between the language of mathematics, exhibited in language proficiency, and computational skills, reflective of academic achievement, has blurred. The National Council of Teachers of Mathematics (NCTM, 2000b) values the explanation of math processes, the description of concepts underlying math operations, the strategies involved in problem solving, and real-world contexts as it does mathematical knowledge. The downside for English language learners, students with disabilities, and other students who struggle with literacy, is that math language often is so dense or contexualized that it masks or impedes students' ability to do the computation to solve the problem.

In the case of large-scale assessment, oftentimes, English language learners must solve math problems through language. Let's examine a released question taken from a state math **test**.

A Grade 3 Item

Twelve children went to the beach. Some of the children went swimming and some played in the sand. There were twice as many children playing in the sand as swimming. How many children were doing each activity?

The language of this item, along with the cultural connotation, can easily be modified without destroying the math operations needed to reach the solution. Using students' everyday experiences and limiting the amount of language, the problem posed above could be changed to the following:

A class has twelve (12) children. There are twice (2X) as many girls as boys. How many girls and boys are there in the class?

Ideally, large-scale assessments should be built from universal design so that all students can use the information appropriately. In addition to managing the language, there are other means of making math problems more accessible to students:

- Creating a glossary (in English and the students' native language)
- Using graphs, charts, tables, or figures
- Bolding key words
- Including line art, diagrams, charts, and tables
- Providing relevant formulas

By maximizing opportunities for English language learners to make meaning from the content, the results from the assessments will be more valid indicators of what the students know academically.

The Language and Content of Science

Scientific inquiry is the bedrock of this content area. Students' language and concepts are expanded through the exploration of scientific phenomena. In the following pair of objectives, teachers can see that the language objective centers on description, whereas the content objective targets measurement within a science context.

Language Proficiency Standard	Academic Content Standard
Language objective for assessment and instruction: *Describe observations orally or in writing as part of scientific inquiry*	Content objective for assessment and instruction: *Use scientific instruments as part of scientific inquiry to make accurate measurements*
Academic language proficiency	Academic achievement

The National Research Council (1996) approaches kindergarten through Grade 12 science education through the study of life sciences, physical sciences, and earth/space sciences. When science is approached as inquiry, students make discoveries firsthand by stating hypotheses, collecting and analyzing data, and drawing conclusions based on the results. While active science is endorsed for all students (Hein & Price, 1994), "learning by doing" for English language learners promotes language and conceptual development simultaneously (Kessler & Quinn, 1987; Mohan, 1986).

In teaching science, as in all content areas, English language learners' level of English language proficiency and academic achievement must be taken into consideration. Just because English language learners may have opportunities to engage in scientific inquiry does not mean that they can process or reproduce the language of science. According to Carrasquillo and Rodríguez (2002), "Science, itself, is a language and each different science is a separate language" (p. 132); therefore, we must prepare our English language learners for the challenge of learning the language and content associated with this discipline.

Teachers must keep in mind that even in science, culture influences our perceptions of the world and it is our responsibility to honor our students' heritage. For example, Native Americans may categorize plants and animals according to their function, whereas formal science uses structure as a classification scheme (Smith, 1986). Through comparison and contrast of cultures, both students and teachers are able to broaden their experiential bases and cross-cultural understanding.

Darian (2003) discusses how the structure, style, and presentation of scientific information can present challenges to English language learners. Therefore, for these students, each step of scientific inquiry should be introduced, reinforced, and reviewed before moving on to the next. Let's think about having students create a hypothesis, the starting point for scientific research. As a teacher, are you asking students to do the following:

- Produce statements or questions
- Create null hypotheses (by making statements using negative terms)

- Use model sentences as templates
- Connect the idea of scientific hypothesis with prediction for language arts

How English language learners respond to each of these approaches requires the use of different language patterns and ways of demonstrating academic language proficiency.

Classroom Instruction and Assessment

Authentic or real-life supports to understand the language and content of science are generally available in schools. For English language learners, these materials are important in making connections from what they may already know in their native language to English. The list in the box below outlines some of the typical kinds of science materials for use in instruction and assessment.

Manipulatives for Science

- Instruments (thermometers, scales, telescopes)
- Physical models (human body, solar system, atoms)
- Natural materials (animals, plants, sponges)
- Actual substances (water, salt, elements)
- Illustrations or graphics of cycles and scientific processes

---

For **classroom assessment** in the area of science, students have the advantage of being able to interact with real-world materials. Students can observe scientific phenomena, illustrate what they see, and draw conclusions either orally or in written form. For young students, the most typical examples include witnessing change by watching seedlings transform into plants; growing mold on bread; making and describing collections, such as leaves, insects, or rocks; or making comparisons over time.

Students in middle grades often construct models, as in replicas of the solar system or atoms. For English language learners, learning is reinforced when they are able to translate information about their models onto charts or analyze the information from charts. By reducing the dependence on print, students are able to process the pertinent information more readily, as in Figure 4.2.

At the high school level, students may use materials for physical science, for instance, to harness solar power, design circuits, or build weight-bearing bridges. To maximize the acquisition of language and content, English language learners should maintain learning logs with illustrations and written text to document what they do and what they learn in class.

Besides actual scientific equipment and materials, videos, as well as other forms of multimedia, are useful instructional assessment tools for English language learners where audio and visual input is combined. For example, after witnessing clips or videos on natural disasters, students new to English may track the pathways of destruction while more proficient students may evaluate, either orally or in writing, their potentially devastating impact. As in all classes, teachers must be sensitive to

Figure 4.2   Using a Chart as a Visual Aid for English Language Learners

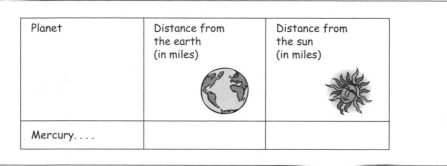

Planet	Distance from the earth (in miles)	Distance from the sun (in miles)
Mercury. . . .		

cultural connections and attuned to students' backgrounds; some English language learners may have witnessed disease (i.e., malaria) and disaster (typhoons, tsunamis) less likely to strike here in the United States and should have opportunities to express their experiences, feelings, and reactions.

Vocabulary Building. Having English as a second language teachers preteach the technical terms and language patterns in English or having bilingual teachers introduce the content vocabulary to the students in their native language will expose English language learners to the language and concepts they will later encounter in general education classrooms. The inspection of scientific instruments or other materials prior to actually conducting an experiment also facilitates students' vocabulary development. Typically, in a classroom, the availability and use of thermometers, scales, magnets, microscopes, telescopes, or other equipment aid in students' discovery of science.

In acquiring basic science vocabulary, English language learners should be encouraged to engage in higher-level thinking to demonstrate comprehension. Students in kindergarten or first grade may choose to compare real fruits and vegetables by color, shape, texture, or presence/absence of seeds (see Appendix 4.2 for a sample activity). These young students may then do a task analysis, such as describing the steps in making a tropical fruit salad. Language proficiency assessment may center on English language learners' use of sequential language, whereas assessment of their academic achievement may have students identify where different kinds of fruits come from or grow.

Differentiating Instruction and Assessment. When instruction is organized into multiple, simultaneous, diversified activities around a central topic that allow students to work toward a variety of goals, it is differentiated (Estrada, 2004). English language learners are a heterogeneous mix of students with differing levels of language proficiency who can benefit from this instructional strategy. Although challenging for teachers to implement, **performance or progress indicators** for each language proficiency level, as shown in Chapter 2, can be extremely useful as the starting point for differentiating instruction and assessment.

English language learners in middle school may engage in scientific inquiry by designing and collecting survey data in small groups of varying language proficiency, summarizing the results, and discussing how the information can be

Table 4.2 Organizing Scientific Inquiry for English Language Learners

The first set of questions is intended for younger students or those with lower levels of English language proficiency. The second set is for older or more proficient English language learners.

The Steps of Scientific Inquiry	*Questions I Need to Answer*
1. Find the problem. (Identify the problem.)	1. What do you want to see? (What are you going to investigate?)
2. Check it out. (Make observations.)	2. What do you see? (What will you examine?)
3. Ask a question. (State your hypothesis.)	3. What do you think is going to happen? (What do you want to explore?)
4. Look for the answer. (Collect data.)	4. What do you need to do? (What information or data do you need?)
5. Describe what you have. (Analyze data.)	5. What did you find out? (What did you discover and what does this information mean?)
6. Explain what happened. (Summarize findings.)	6. What does it tell you? (What does this information tell you?)
7. Answer you question and give reasons. (Draw conclusions.)	7. Why did it happen? (Based on evidence, what is the answer to your question? Support your findings.)

used in practical ways. Assessment of their language proficiency might revolve around their responses to the key questions, such as in Table 4.2. In it, there are two sets of questions for conducting scientific inquiry that address the identical academic content standard but differentiate lower from higher levels of language proficiency.

High school students, irrespective of their **level of language proficiency**, may organize their own taxonomy based on a unit of study. English language learners with limited formal schooling and low levels of literacy can gain a sense of the concept of taxonomy, for example, by classifying labeled pictures of vertebrates/invertebrates or carnivores/herbivores. More proficient English language learners may provide a rationale for the taxonomy and an explanation of how it is arranged. English language learners' control of language or syntactic patterns, quality, quantity, organization of language, and specificity of vocabulary use in science demonstrate their academic language proficiency, whereas the appropriateness of the examples of the taxonomy is the basis for measuring their academic achievement.

Large-Scale Assessment

Large-scale state assessment of science, in large part, remains confined to paper-and-pencil **tasks**. Although students can often refer to diagrams representative of concepts, they cannot discover the solutions firsthand. The cooperative interdependence of students in a lab setting cannot be replicated. As a result, literacy often becomes a confounding variable in the assessment of academic achievement of science.

Those English language learners who have a strong literacy foundation in their native language may readily be able to transfer some technical vocabulary of science. These specialized words may have crept into other languages from English, such as those related to computers, or may be derived from shared Greek or Latin roots, such as medical terms. As part of test preparation, English language learners need to have the strategies in order to make connections between their two languages, such as identifying cognates (August, Calderon, & Gottlieb, 2004; Cummins, 2005).

At other times, students might struggle with words they have encountered in science that also form idiomatic expressions in English. Teachers may need to point out the differences in the use and application of multiple meanings of the words in different contexts. To get a sense of the complexity of the English language, the reflection in Appendix 4.3 has sentences with scientific terms that have corresponding idiomatic expressions that might baffle English language learners.

Differentiation for English language learners should also extend into large-scale assessment. Keeping in mind students' levels of English language proficiency, items should be designed for what students can do. For example, knowing that beginning students can respond only with single words or phrases, **constructed responses** should be visually or graphically supported and require only that amount of discourse. English language learners with higher proficiencies, on the other hand, should be able to generate a series of related sentences or paragraphs.

The Language and Content of Social Studies

The identification of dates, places, people, and events that students encounter in social studies is directly related to content. The description, explanation, and comparison of these entities are the language functions English language learners must acquire to demonstrate their language proficiency. The following example illustrates distinct language and content objectives in the area of social studies.

Language Proficiency Standard	Academic Content Standard
Language objective for assessment and instruction: *Discuss, orally or in writing, a series of historical events using sequential language supported by a timeline*	Content objective for assessment and instruction: *Sequence events by date of occurrence and persons involved*
Academic language proficiency	Academic achievement

For English language learners, the content area of social studies is often fraught with challenges, because many of its concepts fall outside the students' experiential realm. In addition, many themes that thread the U.S. curriculum are abstract in nature. How do you explain "democracy," "justice," "freedom," or "equity" to a refugee child who hasn't had even remote contact with these basic precepts of American history?

As in all learning, we must begin with English language learners' experiential base; connect with their prior knowledge, language, and culture; and expand on what they know. Do teachers realize that the Vietnam War to a Vietnamese student is the American War? Instead of presenting information from a single perspective, seize the teachable moment to probe deeper. In this instance, teachers may ask the students, "Why do you think the war has two names?"

There are instructional strategies, supports, and methods that facilitate English language learners' language development and conceptual understanding. A number of these tools are described within the context of social studies. Chapter 7 has a more detailed explanation of the types of supports that should be afforded second language learners during instruction and assessment.

Classroom Use of Cooperative Learning Structures

English language learners should be encouraged to interact with each other as a means of practicing their new language. Cooperative learning structures (Kagan, 1989) provide that venue for students of varying levels of language proficiency. Incorporated into the classroom routine, these structures are useful for instruction and assessment across the curriculum. Many types of structures can apply across grade and language proficiency levels, including the following:

- Two-way tasks
- Think-pair-share
- Numbered heads together
- Round robin

Cooperative learning may not be familiar for English language learners who have been schooled outside of the United States. Assessment that incorporates cooperative structures should begin with the social and sociocultural skills these students are acquiring in school, such as taking turns, sharing information, and respecting student responses. It also provides ample opportunities for students to engage in **self-** and **peer assessment** within a natural setting.

For two-way tasks, students are paired and each is given different information. Through oral interchange, students question each other to figure out or complete their missing information. In the lower grades, for instance, one student may have a map with a school, post office, and library while a partner has the identical map with other places in the community, such as the police station, hospital, and fire station. Students instruct each other how to locate the places on their specific map. For instance, one student might say to his or her partner, "Go up Main Street to Third Avenue. The police station is on the corner of Main and Third." **Self-assessment** is built into this type of activity as students receive immediate feedback by examining each other's maps at the completion of the activity.

Think-pair-share is similar to brainstorming in that there isn't just one correct answer. Teachers ask probing questions or give instructions: For example, "What are the functions of the U.S. government?" or "List the powers that our government should or should not have," and then allow students thinking time. Students might be paired heterogeneously (such as a shy student with a risk taker, a newly arrived bilingual student with another from the same language background, an English language learner with a native English speaker) or randomly. Students then share their ideas with the class, as the teacher writes the responses on the board.

In numbered heads together, students work in teams (usually of three or four members) where each is assigned a number. The teacher throws out a question, issue, or problem: For example, "How would you change the boundaries of the Middle East so people would live peacefully?" Team members, as a group, discuss the topic and propose possible solutions. When the teacher calls a number, the designated students share their team's information or ideas with the class.

Round robin is another type of cooperative structure where students work in teams or small groups. Here, teachers pose questions that have multiple possible answers: For example, "What are some reasons for prejudice and discrimination?" or "What are the advantages and disadvantages of living in the United States?" Students take turns within their groups either reciting their responses orally or writing them down and passing around a piece of paper to a teammate to write down his or her answer until members of the team have depleted their original thoughts.

Table 4.3 gives examples from social studies of language and content objectives that may be targeted with different types of cooperative structures. It is important that teachers inform students of the objective to be practiced or measured before the activity begins. Student feedback should reflect the language or content objective being assessed.

Use of Graphic and Visual Support for Classroom and Large-Scale Assessment

For English language learners, visual representations are invaluable for acquiring the language and content of social studies. By incorporating these forms of

Table 4.3   Use of Cooperative Structures to Assess Language and Content Social Studies Objectives

Cooperative Structure	Example of the Language of Social Studies (Language Proficiency)	Example of the Content of Social Studies (Academic Achievement)
Two-way tasks	Identify areas of conflict based on directionality	Name and locate specific locales of conflict
Think-pair-share	Select and defend an important right in the Bill of Rights	Name and rank the rights from the Bill of Rights in terms of importance
Numbered heads together	Offer advantages and disadvantages of immigration	Give dates and reasons for and give examples of immigration
Round robin	Use past tense in describing historical eras	Identify features of historical eras from pictures

support into instruction and assessment, teachers can readily facilitate their students' oral language and literacy development.

Manipulatives for Social Studies

- Maps
- Globes
- Arial and satellite photographs
- Timelines
- Atlases
- Compasses
- Multicultural artifacts

Timelines are a form of graphic support that lends itself to social studies and that is useful across **language domains**. Given a series of oral commands, English language learners familiar with this type of organizer can either point to the position on the line or select the appropriate words or phrases from a word wall or bank. Eventually, students can construct their own timelines and give a partner the bank of words, phrases, or even sentences to place in chronological order. In that way, peer assessment is built into the activity.

Because graphic and visual support provides avenues to meaning for English language learners, especially for those with lower levels of language proficiency, it also needs to be incorporated into large-scale assessment. English language learners may not be able to produce an essay on current economic or population trends, but they could readily relate the same concepts by interpreting a graph on demographics. They may not be able to distill the foreign policies of different presidents in written discourse, but they could make comparisons by producing facts on a web or Venn diagram.

Classroom and Large-Scale Assessment Without Visual or Graphic Support

As English language learners become more proficient in English, especially in middle and high school, it is inevitable that they will encounter text without much graphic or visual support. As English language learners approach attainment of English language proficiency, it is important that they work with grade-level material. Teachers still should continue to include instructional adaptations, however, to ensure students' academic success.

With more proficient English language learners, oftentimes, assessment of academic achievement is literacy dependent, such as in the case of cloze exercises. Whereas in the example in Chapter 3, the use of prepositions was being measured for language proficiency, in the following excerpt, the deleted words are vocabulary terms related to third-grade social studies concepts associated with academic achievement.

An Example of a Rationale Cloze Passage With a Word Bank to Assess Academic Achievement

Our Nation's Capital

Washington, D.C., our nation's capital, sits on the East Coast of the United States. It is a city, but not a 1. _____; D.C. stands for District of Columbia. Millions of people come each year to visit its famous 2. _____ and monuments.

The White House is the home of the 3. _____ and his family. The Capitol is the home of Congress; that's where the country's 4. _____are passed. Embassies are homes of foreign diplomats. There are embassies from countries all over the world in Washington, D.C.

Many of the monuments in our nation's capital honor our 5. _____ past presidents. The tallest monument is named for the first president, George Washington. The Lincoln and Jefferson 6. _____ also have the names of important presidents. Our capital is full of beautiful sights.

buildings	country's	state	memorials	President	laws

For measuring academic achievement, teachers may wish to allow even the more proficient English language learners other forms of expression of subject matter knowledge. For example, if the objective is for students to summarize key features of historical periods or geopolitical regions, English language learners may present the information as a series of bullets or in outline form rather than produce a historical essay. If the purpose is to assess language proficiency, and students are to compile research from various sources, then teachers may wish to focus on their use of certain language patterns and technical vocabulary rather than on the historical accuracy of their presentation. In the following writing sample from a sixth grader, it is clear that the student has a firm understanding of voting rights in a democracy (indicative of achievement), yet she uses general rather than specific vocabulary (e.g., *rules* instead of *laws*) and has numerous errors in sentence structure and use of conventions (illustrative of language proficiency).

Vote!

I think wen you are in a free country you have to vote. Some people think is not important. But I will tell you why is important.

First because if you don't vote for your ideas about your country will not count. And you will be unhappy because you want other rules.

Second if you don't vote the president can be bad. And he can put bad rules and you will had to do it.

Some peoples from other country can vote. But some of they don't do it. Then if the president is mean he could said only white people from United States can live hear. And the people from other country will be sorry for not vote.

This is why I think is important to vote. And I hope you can vote.

SUMMARY AND FINAL THOUGHTS

English is a powerful language that often is the only medium of instruction and assessment for English language learners. If English language learners don't have the opportunity to express what they know and are able to do in their native language, their English language proficiency becomes a confounding variable in content area learning. Therefore, it is incumbent on all teachers to be able to differentiate between the language and content of subject matter for language proficiency and academic achievement.

This chapter has created an awareness of some of the complexities involved in English language development that face teachers and their English language learners in the areas of mathematics, science, and social studies, including (1) multiple meanings and applications of a single word (as in the "table" example), (2) a single meaning for multiple terms (as in the addition example), and (3) nuances or subtleness of meaning from word order. Use of sound instructional strategies and supports can be a springboard to valid classroom assessment. Thus the daunting task of preparing English language learners for large-scale assessment may be offset, in part, by having collected a body of evidence that distinguishes English language proficiency from academic achievement. Multiple data sources, derived from classroom and large-scale efforts, provide a more complete and accurate picture of our students' performance in school.

APPENDIX 4.1

Features Associated With Assessment of Language and Content Across the Curriculum

Teachers may use this chart as a checklist in designing content-based lessons or units of instruction and assessment for their English language learners. The language features are geared to promoting language proficiency, and the content features address academic achievement.

		Language Arts	Mathematics	Science	Social Studies
L A N G U A G E	Language focus/objective				
	Use of language functions				
	Use of specialized or technical language				
	Language complexity or density				
	Communication/ language patterns				
	Cross-cultural connections				
C O N T E N T	Anchored in English language proficiency standards				
	Content focus/objective				
	Skill attainment				
	Conceptual knowledge				
	Comprehension of concepts				
	Anchored in academic content standards				

APPENDIX 4.2

A Sample Listening Assessment Activity for Young English Language Learners

English Language Proficiency Standard, Model Performance Indicator for Science, Listening, English language proficiency Levels 1 through 3 (State of Wisconsin, 2004):

Identify, match, or group objects according to chemical or physical properties from pictures and oral statements.

Teacher Directions: Prior to the activity, make packets of the ten pictures (for children who are acquiring literacy, you may wish to provide the words underneath). As part of the instructional cycle, students may be introduced to actual fruits and vegetables, plastic replicas, or pictures from magazines. As you describe the characteristics of individual fruits or vegetables, students hold up the corresponding picture or pair of pictures.

As an extension of this listening activity, young students at the lower proficiency levels may partner and orally share the names of the fruits and vegetables according to the different classification schemes. They may then, in partners, create a composite attribute list, either orally or in writing; for example, "A cucumber—it's green, smooth, long, has seeds, and is a vegetable."

| An orange | Green chilies | Yellow bananas | A red apple | An ear of yellow corn |
| Purple grapes | Red potatoes | An orange pumpkin | A purple eggplant | A green cucumber |

APPENDIX 4.3

REFLECTION: Multiple Meanings

English language learners struggle with the myriad multiple meanings in our language. The following vocabulary words represent common science terms, as shown in the sentences in the right-hand column. However, all these words also form multiple idiomatic expressions. Think about how each of these terms can be used in different ways and write your responses in the column to the left; then pool your answers with other teachers.

Vocabulary	Idiomatic Expressions	Science Terms
Ear		(N) My *ear* is blocked.
Cold		(N) I have a *cold.* (ADJ) Ice is *cold*
Flame		(N) The *flame* was intense.
Chain		(N) Animals form a food *chain.*
Palm		(ADJ) *Palm* trees are beautiful. (N) I caught the ball in the *palm* of my hand
Rock		(N) Geology is the study of *rocks.*
Star		(N) The *stars* are brilliant tonight.
Light		(N) The *light* shone in the window. (ADJ) A feather is *light.*
Cells		(N) *Cells* are the smallest unit of life.
Heat		(V) We *heat* our homes with oil.

5

Classroom Assessment

The Bridge to Educational Parity

Education is all a matter of building bridges.

—Ralph Ellison

As educators, we are bombarded with opportunities to assess our students. But what exactly does **assessment** entail? This chapter explains the complex nature of assessment and the choices that teachers must make to implement sound assessment practices. It attempts to clarify some misunderstandings that surround assessment and pose some sound solutions to nagging issues. Most important, it asserts that the development and use of viable assessments for **English language learners** will facilitate the building of a bridge to educational parity so that they may enjoy the educational benefits afforded their English proficient peers.

THE DISTINCTIONS BETWEEN TESTING, ASSESSMENT, AND EVALUATION

These three terms, often interchangeable in our daily discussions, actually represent quite different constructs. **Testing** is a systematic procedure of collecting a sample of student behavior at one point in time. Assessment is a comprehensive process of planning, collecting, analyzing, reporting, and using information on students over time. Assessment can include tests as well as **projects,** anecdotal information, and student self-reflection. **Evaluation** is broadest in scope involving a methodical process whereby assessment information on students or programs is used to make evidence-based decisions from informed judgment. Figure 5.1 shows the relationships between these three related terms (TESOL, 1998).

Figure 5.1   Evaluation, Assessment, and Testing: Three Forms of Collecting, Analyzing, and Reporting Information

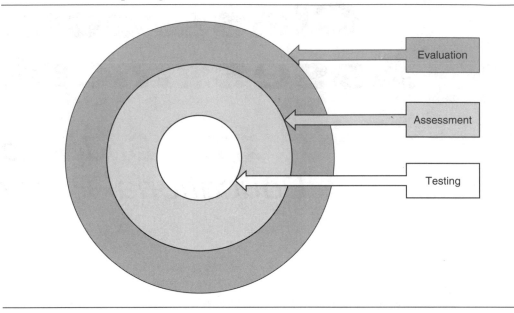

Our discussion in this book centers on assessment. Assessment implies relying on **multiple measures** or data sources, gathering information at multiple data points (a span of time); involving multiple stakeholders, perhaps for a variety of purposes; and using the accumulated information to improve student learning and teaching. Continuous feedback ensures that data are constantly being updated to provide the most relevant and accurate information for decision making.

In Chapter 1, we saw that initial identification of English language learners and their placement into appropriate instructional programs depends on assessment data. We also have seen numerous ways of approaching the assessment of **language proficiency** and **academic achievement**. The reliance on multiple data sources or measures is equally important at the classroom and large-scale levels.

IMPLEMENTING CLASSROOM ASSESSMENT

We approach assessment from two perspectives. **Classroom assessment**, which reflects the ongoing learning environment, includes activities, **tasks**, and projects embedded in instruction for the primary purpose of monitoring student progress. This type of assessment is generally performance based, where the students are actively involved. Thus, in the classroom, students engage in ongoing discussion; construct models, figures, and maps; conduct science experiments; delve into technology; self-assess their accomplishments; apply strategies; or create original pieces through process writing. **Performance assessment** requires a set of well-articulated criteria, grounded in standards that are shared with students, such as through **rubrics** or scoring guides. The same set of criteria, if used over time, allows teachers and students to monitor and profile students' language learning.

Classroom assessment complements and contributes to **large-scale assessment**. All standardized measures—namely, **norm-referenced** and **criterion-referenced tests**—fall into the large-scale category. However, some states and school districts incorporate direct writing and open-ended responses into their large-scale measures. Thus the emphasis on standards-based instruction and assessment has tended to blur, to some extent, the distinction between classroom and large-scale efforts to measure students' achievement.

Both classroom and large-scale assessment are vital to education today. English language learners must demonstrate acquisition of the language and the concepts of the content areas through assessment of English language proficiency and academic achievement. These two venues provide teachers with different types of information for decision making. Appendix 5.1 illustrates how each contributes to painting a picture of English language learners.

As educators, we must be attentive to how our students learn and how they demonstrate their learning; therefore, it is our responsibility to provide English language learners with the appropriate tools and techniques to enable them to thrive within a standards-based environment. On the other hand, we must be aware of how assessment operates outside our individual classrooms—at a grade level or at department, district, or state levels—and its subsequent impact on our English language learners. The next section presents an organizing framework for assessment and describes its classroom application.

Organization of Classroom Assessment

English language learners, by definition, need language support that is built from and connected to their prior linguistic, cultural, and educational experiences. To that end, curriculum, instruction, and assessment should serve as a springboard or scaffold from students' previous exposure to language and content to new contexts. The most effective way of introducing this scaffolding is through a series of interrelated instructional assessment activities that fold into tasks, which, in turn, shape projects.

An assessment scheme is presented in Figure 5.2; it depicts a series of nested figures that show how questions and activities are embedded in tasks that, in turn, form the basis for projects. This classification illustrates how instruction and assessment can be organized, with each successive category representing a more complex performance. Assessments can be designed from questions to projects, using multiple measures from a single category or a combination of categories.

Figure 5.2   The Relationships Between Questions, Activities, Tasks, and Projects as the
Basis for Instruction and Assessment

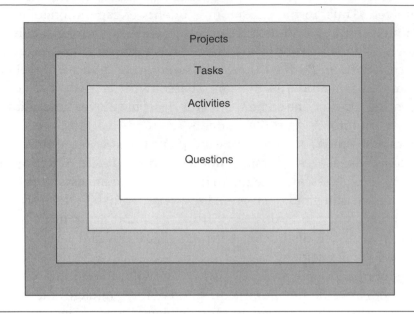

Questions are the most discrete of the categories; they may be asked in isolation or grouped together. Activities composed of a set of interrelated questions or a single, in-depth question often center on a learning objective taken from one standard within one **language domain** or content area. Two or more activities combine to create a task. A task, by consisting of multiple activities, is broader in both scope and depth. As one **activity** builds on the next one, generally, higher levels of cognitive engagement are possible with tasks than with activities.

Projects are the most long-ranged in duration, perhaps corresponding with a unit of study, and may involve several tasks. Theme-based, or interdisciplinary instruction across the content areas, allows students to explore issues and probe in-depth topics. The reflection in Appendix 5.2 gives examples of the different activities, tasks, and projects used for instructional assessment within a classroom setting.

Both classroom, or instructional assessment, and large-scale assessment can consist of these various categories. Although large-scale assessment is mainly confined to questions and activities, the more performance-based it is, the more it can lean toward more comprehensive projects. So, for example, a school or school district may rely on a project-based portfolio, double-scored by teachers using a uniform rubric, to supplement its **standardized test** scores. Some states have dabbled in the use of student portfolios as part of their educational reform initiatives (Gottlieb, 2002; Guskey, 1994; Murphy & Underwood, 2000).

Defining the Scope of Tasks and Projects for Classroom Assessment

Two dimensions define the parameters of a task or project: (1) its breadth, or overall coverage, and (2) its depth, or degree of comprehensiveness. These dimensions and the factors associated with each, outlined in Appendix 5.3, are to be taken into account in planning classroom assessment (Gottlieb, 2002). The breadth of a task or project is contingent on *who* is involved and *what* amount of time is needed. Is it being created only for English language learners or for all students? Is it to represent a collaborative effort by a team of teachers, or will it be designed by the bilingual/ESL teacher? How many class periods have to be allocated for instructional assessment?

The depth of a task or project reflects *what* is required and *how* extensive is its representation. What are the language and **content objectives,** and how are they reflected in state English language proficiency and **academic content standards**? Does scaffolding allow for increased linguistic complexity that challenges English language learners across language proficiency levels? Are various cognitive targets attainable for English language learners through graphic or visual support? Finally, are there ways built into the instructional assessment so that all English language learners can demonstrate their language proficiency or knowledge and conceptual understanding?

English language learners come in all ages from a variety of linguistic and cultural backgrounds. The breadth and depth of tasks and projects must match the characteristics of students served in your classroom or school. If you are in a high school with large numbers of students with limited formal education or interrupted schooling, tasks and projects would be crafted differently than for students who have had continuous education in their **native language**. Likewise, if you are in an elementary school serving English language learners with disabilities, your curriculum, although representative of the same standards, would assume different dimensions of breadth and depth.

Features of Classroom Assessment

Activities, tasks, and projects should form the core of classroom assessment where English language learners can produce creative and varied responses to challenging questions, issues, or problems. The teachers' use of a template as a guide for instructional assessment allows for joint planning, delivery of lessons, and interpretation of student work. Some of the features to consider in the instructional assessment sequence include the following:

- The integration of instruction, assessment, and documentation of evidence
- Measurement of multiple standards within and across language domains and content areas
- Appropriateness for a range of language proficiency levels in English (and the native language)
- Incorporation of students' multicultural, experiential, and educational backgrounds
- Visual or graphic support, such as the use of graphic organizers, to enhance meaning
- Performance that leads to original student work
- Diverse avenues for producing student work

Figure 5.3   Standards-Based Education of English Language Learners

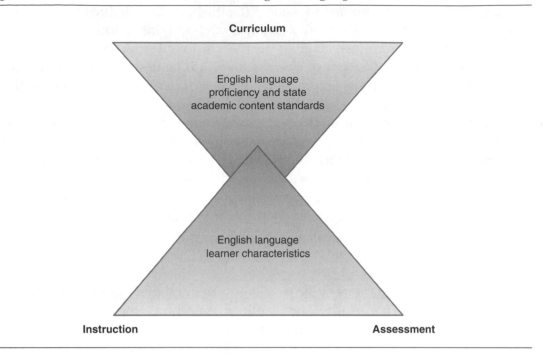

- Flexibility of use in a variety of settings and a variety of teaching methodologies
- Varied time for implementation (Gottlieb, 2002)

To summarize, standards-based education begs a connection between curriculum, instruction, and assessment. This **alignment** has to hold true for both classroom and large-scale assessment practices. In addition, characteristics unique to English language learners (see Chapter 1) must be integrated into a model, such as the one shown in Figure 5.3.

Preparation for Classroom Assessment

So where do we begin in preparation for classroom assessment of English language learners? There are numerous schemes for organizing curriculum, instruction, and assessment. One such way is to envision a four-phase process:

- Phase 1: planning
- Phase 2: delivery
- Phase 3: interpretation of the results
- Phase 4: use of results for feedback

This instructional assessment cycle is graphically depicted in Figure 5.5 (later in this chapter).

Developing instructional assessment tasks and projects is an arduous undertaking. It is advisable that bilingual/ESL teachers work in collaboration with their grade-level or department colleagues. Coordination of teacher effort can result in a workable and common format for developing instructional assessment that can be used throughout the academic year and beyond.

Designing units of instructional assessment based on tasks or projects should be part of teachers' professional development; consultants and curriculum coordinators should work alongside grade-level groups to construct exemplary products. The criteria associated with quality instructional assessment projects and tasks are listed in Appendix 5.4; this **checklist** may be useful to share with teacher groups involved in curriculum development for English language learners.

Designing Classroom Assessment

In this section, we will explore "Weather Around the World," a project created for middle school that could be adapted for primary grades, as an illustrative example of classroom-based instructional assessment. It has been created for all students, with emphasis on English language learners, and represents a collaborative effort by a team of content and language teachers. A blank template for personal use is found in Appendix 5.5, and a completed template of the instructional assessment sequence for this project is presented in Appendix 5.6.

Planning

In planning classroom assessment for English language learners, we (1) select academic content and **language proficiency standards**, (2) formulate content and **language objective**s, (3) match the content and language to the tasks or project, and (4) align assessment measures with instruction. Remember that for English language learners, content is the primary vehicle to academic achievement while language reflects English language proficiency. In the planning phase, we name the project and identify its burning issue or "big idea"—in this case, "Variations in weather patterns affect how people live."

Content

National and state academic content area standards for this project can be drawn from the areas of science, mathematics, social studies, and language arts. In particular, the following divisions are used as the source for identifying the specific standards and performance indicators that would apply:

- Science: physical world or science applications
- Mathematics: probability and statistics
- Social studies: geography
- Language arts: writing

For each discipline, content objectives are then developed that focus on the specific academic skills of the project. Objectives are written as clear, measurable behaviors that mirror the standards addressed. The following is an example of content objectives for this weather project.

English language learners will

- Science: identify and chart weather patterns
- Mathematics: use descriptive statistics to calculate weather patterns
- Social Studies: compare weather patterns in two different locations, drawing from cultural heritage
- Language arts: summarize results of the study of weather patterns and apply to own lives

The next step in designing instruction and assessment is determining which **language functions**, language patterns, and vocabulary use are associated with the varying levels of English language proficiency and content objectives. English language proficiency standards are the source document for formulating the language objectives.

Language

For this weather project, English language learners will interact using all the language domains (listening, speaking, reading, and writing); however, we will concentrate on assessing the productive areas of speaking and writing. Language objectives complement content objectives; the integration of language and content within delivery provides comprehensible input for the students. Examples of language objectives are provided below for each level of English language proficiency, starting with the lowest. English language learners, at their given **level of language proficiency**, will do the following:

Level 1

- Identify, by pointing, different kinds of weather illustrations
- Match vocabulary to examples of descriptive statistics
- Sort visually supported weather patterns by location
- List results from classifying weather patterns

Level 2

- Identify and copy visually or graphically supported weather patterns from TV or newspapers
- Match vocabulary with definitions to descriptive statistics
- List key elements of weather patterns in two different locations
- Produce phrases and short sentences about key elements of visually or graphically supported weather patterns and their personal relevance

Level 3

- Identify and record on a chart visually supported weather patterns from newspapers and the Internet
- Describe use of descriptive statistics related to weather patterns
- Compare visually supported weather patterns in two different locations, using a graphic diagram

- Produce an illustrated paragraph stating results of the study of weather patterns from a personal perspective

Level 4

- Identify and chart weather patterns from various visually or graphically supported sources
- Show how descriptive statistics relate to weather patterns
- Construct a graphic organizer and compare weather patterns in two different locations
- Produce multiple paragraphs discussing results of the study and describe personal effects of weather patterns from information from the chart.

Level 5

- Identify and chart weather patterns from grade-level texts
- Use information from descriptive statistics to explain weather patterns
- Compare weather patterns in two different locations, using data collected over time
- Summarize results in a report on the study of weather patterns from information from the chart and apply to own lives

The selection of the language for instruction and assessment is part of the planning process. To meet content objectives, native language instruction or support is suggested, especially for those English language learners who are literate in their first language or who participate in dual language programs. Obviously, for language objectives that reflect English language proficiency standards, the medium of instruction and assessment is English.

RELECTION: Examining Language and Content Objectives

There are many different ways to organize instructional assessment based on standards. What is critical for English language learners is that the language objectives target English language proficiency and that content objectives center on academic achievement, either in the native language or in English. Read over the objectives on the weather project. How might you change them for the English language learners with whom you work? Discuss how you might approach the language and content of this unit with another teacher.

Types of Assessment

Assessment for this project is performance based and embedded in instruction. The products or student work samples determine which types of documentation are most appropriate. In this instance, English language learners will be producing an oral or written report and an essay or speech (depending on their level of English language proficiency) with accompanying graphics, charts, graphic organizers, or perhaps a map. Technology could also be incorporated by having the students explore and reference Internet sites where weather information is obtained. These oral or written student work samples will be interpreted with holistic oral language or writing rubrics.

Content assessment entails geographic precision in map design, math calculations using descriptive statistics, and scientific accuracy of weather events. For measuring content, a **rating scale** will be used.

The information regarding the responsibilities of students for learning language and content should be shared with the students beforehand. Presenting this in the form of a project guide gives English language learners a reference, enabling them to understand the parameters of their assignments. In addition, the learning objectives can be incorporated into a form for student **self-assessment** at the end of the project. (More details regarding rubrics, scoring guides, and student self-assessment are in Chapters 6 and 7.)

Delivery

In the next phase, teachers define the activities within the tasks that the students will engage in. Each task has a product or student work sample that is the basis for language and content assessment. The types of **supports** for English language learners are also noted; they include the materials and resources available to the students to facilitate learning.

Before instructional assessment begins, teachers decide how the students are grouped. Each activity is designated as one for small groups, pairs, or individuals.

Interpreting Results

Peer or student self-assessment promotes student involvement in their own learning and provides built-in monitoring of their progress. English language learners can be taught to maintain an illustrated learning log where they note one or two new concepts or language patterns after each activity. They may also use a checklist to pace their learning.

Teachers can provide students a product descriptor with a timeline for each activity and its associated product. The project descriptor can be readily converted into an analytic rubric with assigned points, such as in Appendix 5.7, which could then be used for grading purposes. In the reporting summary, language is separated from content so that English language learners gain a sense of their accomplishments on both dimensions.

Feedback and Use of Information

In this final phase of instructional assessment, students have opportunities to apply their new skills by viewing each other's projects and offering feedback to one another, following a standard format, such as the project descriptor list.

Teachers respond to students' learning log entries on an ongoing basis and give constructive advice. In addition, teacher-student conferences can be held to promote interaction and bring closure to the project.

Other Forms of Data Collection Within a Classroom Environment

Quizzes, tests, and performance assessments are not the only means teachers use to collect information on students. Conferences or interviews with students yield much insight into students' attitudes, motivation, and effort, as well as performance. These approaches, including teacher observation, are especially effective for young learners and English language learners at the beginning levels of English language proficiency who have to demonstrate their understanding in nontraditional ways.

Teacher Observation

Teacher observation is a powerful tool that is an important form of ongoing classroom assessment. Teachers are constantly "kid watching"; it may be spontaneous, such as when seizing the teachable moment, or planned in advance. Anecdotal information can be collected (traditionally, by note taking or perhaps with handheld technology) when students are interacting with each other or when approached individually by the teacher.

Teachers should observe a few students at a time. In the weather project, for example, teachers may want to concentrate on assessing their English language learners at the beginning levels of English language proficiency. Table 5.1 takes the language objectives and converts them into a checklist where each column is an individual

Table 5.1 Converting Language Objectives Into a Checklist for Beginning English Language Learners

Level 1 English Language Learners	AB	BC	CD	DE	EF
Identify, by pointing, different kinds of weather					
Match vocabulary to examples of descriptive statistics					
Sort weather patterns by location					
List results from classifying weather patterns					
Level 2 English Language Learners	GH	HI	IJ	JK	KL
Identify and copy weather patterns from TV or newspapers					
Match vocabulary with definitions to descriptive statistics					
List key elements of weather patterns in two different locations					
Produce phrases and short sentences about key elements of weather patterns and their personal relevance					

student (represented by two letters, as in Abigail Benitez for AB, Boris Crikowski for BC, and so on). As the activities proceed and students are given opportunities to show that they are meeting the objectives, teachers mark the appropriate box with an X or the date. In addition, teachers can write more qualitative information on student note cards, perhaps placed in alphabetical order on a clipboard underneath the checklist.

Types of Student Responses in Classroom and Large-Scale Assessment

Students may provide assessment data in many different forms, depending on the activity, task, or project. Often, several types of response are required in extended, complex instructional assessment. Figure 5.4 presents a range of available response types by students, from the most to least restrictive.

Figure 5.4   The Range of Response Types in Student Assessment

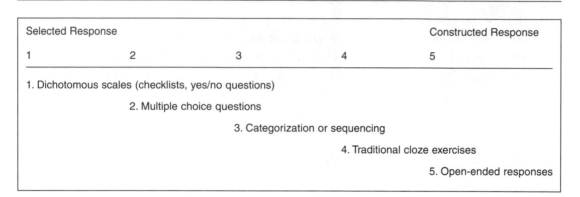

Selected Response   Constructed Response

1   2   3   4   5

1. Dichotomous scales (checklists, yes/no questions)
    2. Multiple choice questions
        3. Categorization or sequencing
            4. Traditional cloze exercises
                5. Open-ended responses

Types of Selected Response

In **selected response**, all possible answers are listed for the students. Dichotomous scales offer students two choices, such as in true/false or yes/no questions or perhaps classification of pictures or words. A checklist is another example of a dichotomous scale.

Selected response also refers to responses that involve multiple choice, categorization, or sequencing where the number of possible options for students is expanded to three or four. For categorization, in the area of mathematics, English language learners may be asked to read some problems and decide which operation to use: addition, subtraction, multiplication, or division. For sequencing, in the area of social studies, English language learners may be asked to sort phrases or sentences as to whether the event described occurred before, during, or after the Civil War.

Cloze exercises, a form of reading comprehension assessment where discourse level text has blanks inserted where words have been removed, are another example of selected response. Chapters 3 and 4 show how cloze exercises are useful for assessing language proficiency or academic achievement. For beginning English language learners, it is advantageous to have either multiple-choice answers for a cloze exercise or a bank of words from which the students select the appropriate responses. In either case, these English language learners would have textual support and are not forced to retrieve words from memory. More advanced English language learners would be required, on the other hand, to respond in the more traditional way and supply their own words.

Types of Constructed Response

Constructed response provides the most latitude for students by allowing them to produce original work and to be innovative and creative in approaching complex issues. With open-ended responses, there can be multiple solutions to questions or acceptance of various perspectives. Constructed response for English language learners, depending on their level of English language proficiency, may entail illustrating and labeling a math problem to producing a persuasive essay.

Obviously, scoring is easy when there is only one correct answer, and **reliability** is greater with selected response. However, English language learners, as all students, should also have opportunities to demonstrate deep learning, and that can be accomplished only through performance-based instruction and assessment, such as in the weather project. Chapter 6 discusses the documentation and interpretation of results of standards-based performance assessment through the use of rubrics. It also addresses how to use assessment information for feedback and decision making.

SUMMARY AND FINAL THOUGHTS

This chapter focuses on the features of standards-based assessment and how teachers design and implement activities, tasks, and projects for their English language learners in classroom or in large-scale contexts. Figure 5.5 is a graphic summary of the cyclical nature of the assessment process. The starting point in the assessment of English language learners is selecting English language proficiency and state academic content standards used to frame language and content objectives. These, along with student and program features, are taken into consideration in the planning phase.

Embedded in instructional assessment, evidence is systematically gathered, organized, and analyzed. Standards-referenced results are used to inform various stakeholders, including students and parents. This information reveals how students are performing in relation to the standards and provides feedback to teachers.

Information from classroom assessment is as valuable as that gained through large-scale endeavors. By designing a rigorous, standards-driven curriculum, delivering it through rich, **content-based instruction**, and assessing student performance comprehensively, teachers of English language learners can engage in exemplary practices. At the same time, given continuity in educational experiences and program support, English language learners will be afforded enhanced opportunities to reach parity with their English proficient peers.

Figure 5.5 The Assessment Cycle in a Standards-based Educational System

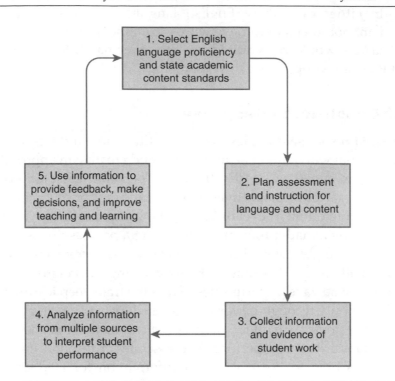

SOURCE: Adapted from TESOL (1998).

APPENDIX 5.1

The Measurement of English Language Proficiency and Academic Achievement at the Classroom and Large-Scale Levels

	Classroom Assessment	*Large-Scale Assessment*
English language proficiency . . . grounded in English language proficiency standards	Ongoing English as a second language (ESL) curriculum-based assessment of listening, speaking, reading, and writing, as embedded in instruction	Standardized English language proficiency testing across the four language domains on an annual basis
Academic achievement . . . grounded in state academic content standards	Ongoing school, district, or state curriculum-based assessment of content and concepts delivered through sheltered means in L2 or in L1	Standardized testing in the content areas—language arts, math, science, and social studies—through alternate or accommodated means in L2 or L1

APPENDIX 5.2

REFLECTION: Questions, Activities, Tasks, or Projects

Have you used any of these questions, activities, tasks, or projects for instruction and assessment? Think about how you would categorize the different types of instructional assessment for English language learners in your classroom. You may share what you do with other teachers at your grade level and think about how you might embed questions, activities, and tasks into richer projects. (Answers follow.)

---

1. _____ Responding to oral commands

2. _____ Contributing samples to a journal

3. _____ Constructing a model along with a chart of its statistics

4. _____ Producing a process-writing piece

5. _____ Conducting a survey and graphing the results

6. _____ Solving a series of math problems and explaining the answers

7. _____ Writing an essay using information gathered from multiple sources on the Internet

8. _____ Creating an illustrated brochure

9. _____ Comparing and contrasting two stories, articles, or works

10. _____ Completing a lab worksheet

REFLECTION Answers for Questions, Activities, Tasks, or Projects

1. *Questions;* 2. *Activity;* 3. *Project;* 4. *Project;* 5. *Task;* 6. *Questions;* 7. *Project;* 8. *Project;* 9. *Task;* 10. *Activity*

APPENDIX 5.3

The Parameters of Classroom Assessment

Breadth of a Task or Project →	*Depth of a Task or Project* ↓
• Number of students involved • Number of teachers/classrooms involved • Number of grade levels involved • Time allocation • Language(s) of instruction	• Number of language domains represented • Number of content areas represented • Number of standards represented • Range of linguistic complexity, according to levels of language proficiency • Range of cognitive involvement • Range of conceptual knowledge

APPENDIX 5.4

A Review Sheet for Instructional Assessment of Projects and Tasks for English Language Learners

Name of project or task: _____

Grade level(s): _____

The Project or Task	YES	NO*
1. Covers a representative sample of English language proficiency or academic content standards		
2. Adequately reflects the standards in scope and breadth		
3. Exemplifies grade level curriculum		
4. Makes provision for multiple language proficiency levels		
5. Requires student work samples or products for the language domains or content area(s) addressed		
6. Offers a realistic time frame for implementation		
7. Is authentic and appropriate for the students' age		
8. Follows a logical sequence of scaffolded activities		
9. Contains visual or graphic support that reduces dependency on print		
10. Allows for differentiation of instruction and assessment		

*For every "no" response, offer a suggestion on how to enhance the task or project.

APPENDIX 5.5

A Template for a Classroom Instructional Assessment Project

Name of the project: _____

Burning issue or big idea: _____

Teachers involved (ESL, bilingual, general education): _____

Grade level or grade-level cluster(s): K 1 2 3 4 5 6 7 8 9 10 11 12

Duration of project: _____

I. *Planning: The Parameters for Assessment*
   A. Content
      1. Content area(s), academic content standards, and performance indicators assessed:

         Mathematics _____ Science _____ Social Studies _____
         Language Arts/Reading _____

      2. Content objectives: _____

      3. Language(s) of instruction and assessment: English _____
         Spanish _____ Other _____

   B. Language
      1. Language domains, English language proficiency standards, and performance indicators assessed:

         Listening _____ Speaking _____ Reading _____ Writing _____

      2. Language objectives: _____

      3. Targeted levels of English language proficiency: _____

   C. Type(s) of Assessment: _____

      1. Product(s) or student work sample(s): _____

      2. Type(s) of student response(s): _____

      3. Materials or resources (visual or graphic support): _____

         _____

      4. Type(s) of documentation (rubric) or scoring guide(s): _____

II. *Delivering: The Instructional Assessment Sequence for a Project*

Task 1

Grouping of students: Individuals _____ Pairs _____ Small groups _____

Description of what students do:

Activity 1.1

Activity 1.2

Task 2

Grouping of students: Individuals _____ Pairs _____ Small groups _____

Description of what students do:

Activity 2.1

Activity 2.2

III. *Interpreting Results*

Peer or student self-assessment: _____

Teacher assessment: _____

IV. *Feedback and Use of Information*

From peer or student self-assessment: _____

From rubrics or documentation forms: _____

From teachers: _____

APPENDIX 5.6

A Completed Template for a Classroom Instructional Assessment Project

Name of the project: Weather Around the World

Burning issue or big idea: Variations in weather patterns affect how people live

Teachers involved (ESL, bilingual, general education): A middle school team of teachers

Grade level or grade-level cluster(s): 5-8

Duration of project: Two to four weeks

- I. *Planning: The parameters for assessment*
  - A. Content
    1. Content area **strands**, academic content standards, and performance indicators assessed:
       - Mathematics—statistics and probability
       - Science—physical world
       - Social studies—geography: people, places, and environment
       - Language arts—writing
    2. Content objectives
       - Science: identify and chart weather patterns
       - Mathematics: use descriptive statistics to define weather patterns
       - Social studies: compare weather patterns in two different locations, drawing from cultural heritage, by applying information from charts or tables
       - Language arts: summarize results of the study of weather patterns and their impact on student lives
    3. Language(s) of instruction and assessment: English and native language

  - B. Language
    1. Language domains, English language proficiency standards, and performance indicators assessed: See details as outlined by language proficiency level in Chapter 5.
    2. Language objectives
       - Listening
         - o Watch videos, TV news and note information
         - o Provide information to peers by pointing or role playing
       - Speaking
         - o Ask and answer questions
         - o Compare and contrast information
         - o Summarize and interpret information
       - Reading

- Locate information in reference materials
- Compare information from different sources
- Writing
  - Design or complete a graphic organizer
  - Summarize and interpret information
  - Produce a poster or report

3. Targeted levels of English language proficiency: All

II. *Delivering: The Instructional Assessment Sequence for a Project*
   A. Task 1: Designing and Describing a Topographic Map
      1. Type(s) of language assessment: written or oral summary
      2. Product(s) or content-based work sample(s): topographic map
      3. Documentation: checklist based on requirements of Activities 1.1 and 1.2
      4. Materials or resources: atlas or access to Internet; materials for map making

Activity 1.1:
Grouping of students: pairs or small groups
Students will

- Choose a state or country
- Use the Internet or an atlas to define its physical features (size, land forms, and bodies of water)
- Reproduce or construct a topographical map to scale
- Label the physical features of the map
- Add longitude and latitude lines
- Identify major cities and capitals

Activity 1.2
Grouping of students: individuals and pairs
Students will

- Write a summary or orally summarize their state or country
- Include information of the place's physical and geographic features from Activity 1.1
- Compare and contrast their place's physical and geographic features with those of a peer

   B. Task 2: Charting Weather Patterns
      1. Type(s) of language assessment: report (written or oral)
      2. Product(s): double entry bar graph with calculations
      3. Documentation: for language proficiency—rating scale on asking questions, making comparisons, summarizing results, and interpreting information; for academic achievement—accuracy of calculations
      4. Materials or resources: Internet, newspapers, or newscasts

Activity 2.1:
Grouping of students: individuals
Students will

- Keep a record of daytime highs and lows for their special place for 10 consecutive days
- Note any form and quantity of precipitation
- Chart results from the record sheet to produce a double entry bar graph
- Formulate questions about their chart and compare results with those of a peer

Activity 2.2:
Grouping of students: individuals
Students will

- Calculate descriptive statistics for the data set, including
  - ✓ mean daytime, nighttime, and overall temperature
  - ✓ median temperatures (day, night, combined)
  - ✓ modes (day, night, combined)
  - ✓ range of temperatures
  - ✓ frequency distribution of temperatures

- Summarize and interpret information to produce a weather report

C. Task 3: Analyzing a Severe Weather Event
   1. Type of language assessment: essay or poster on "How Weather Changes Peoples' Lives"
   2. Product(s) or content-based work sample(s): photojournal or poster, graphic organizer
   3. Documentation: task-specific rubric on language and content of Activities 3.1 and 3.2
   4. Materials or resources: magazines, Internet, videos

Activity 3.1:
Grouping of students: individual or pairs
Students will

- Research and find a minimum of two articles and photographs or videos on a severe weather event that could affect their state or country
- Read and highlight the information or watch videos and take notes
- Complete a graphic organizer (such as a T chart) that lists the characteristics of the weather event and its consequences or impact on people and their community

Activity 3.2 (culminating activity):
Grouping of students: individuals
Students will

- Write an essay or produce a poster with sentences that illustrates the effects of a severe weather event on the people and their homes in their state or country.
- In the essay or poster, identify and describe a particular scientific tool or technology that has changed or could change the effects of this weather disaster.
- Explain how the tool or technology could make life better for the people living there.

III. *Interpreting Results*

Peer or student self-assessment

- Incorporate peer review into the culminating activity
- Have students maintain a learning log throughout the project

Teacher assessment

- Provide students a product descriptor with a timeline for the activities (the project descriptor can be converted to an analytic rubric with assigned points for each component, such as in Appendix 5.7)
- Use a holistic project rubric

IV. *Feedback and Use of Information*

From peer or student self-assessment: Students view each other's projects, set up as a fair around the room, and provide feedback to one another, following a standard form.

From rubrics or documentation forms: The project descriptor is shared and discussed with students as each activity is introduced.

From teachers: Teachers respond to students' journal entries. Teacher-student conferences are planned at the end of the project or marking period.

APPENDIX 5.7

*Summary of Grading and Reporting Task 1
of the "Weather Around the World" Project*

Task		Activities	Possible Points
1: Designing and describing a topographic map	**C O N T E N T**	• Choose a state or country • Use the Internet or an atlas to define its physical features (size, land forms, and bodies of water) • Reproduce or construct a topographical map to scale • Label the physical features of the map • Add longitude and latitude lines • Identify major cities and capitals	5 20 45 10 10 10
	Geography		Total Points out of 100
	L A N G U A G E	• Write a summary or orally summarize their state or country • Include information of the place's physical and geographic features (from Activity 1.1) • Compare and contrast their place's physical and geographic features with those of a peer	50 20 30
	Speaking **Writing**		Total Points out of 100

6

Documenting Performance Assessment

The Bridge From Teachers to Classrooms

I have not been by that bridge . . . without yearning to cross it.

—Mark Twain

RATIONALE FOR PERFORMANCE ASSESSMENT FOR ENGLISH LANGUAGE LEARNERS

English **language proficiency standards**, along with **academic content standards**, lend themselves to countless instructional **assessment** activities, tasks, and projects. **Performance assessment**, where students express their learning in direct ways that reflect real-life situations, is integral to the classroom routine. Because performance assessment connects students' experiences with the curriculum through active involvement, the assessment itself is part of the learning process.

Participation of **English language learners** in performance assessment, irrespective of their levels of English language proficiency, is advantageous. Hands-on assessment allows second language learners to do the following:

- Use multiple modalities to express themselves, such as through actions, oral expression, or in writing, rather than being confined to paper-and-pencil tasks
- Incorporate the identical support materials, such as visuals, graphics, and manipulatives, used for instruction
- Work and interact with partners or in small groups
- Reinforce learning through scaffolding previous educational and personal experiences

In the previous chapter, we laid out how **activities, tasks,** and **projects** shape classroom instruction and assessment. Scoring guides and **rubrics** are the primary tools for documenting these performances. This chapter expands on the notion of performance assessment for English language learners and discusses the pros and cons of rubric use.

THE NATURE OF PERFORMANCE ASSESSMENT

The many forms of performance assessment run the gamut from a set of unrelated activities to comprehensive, in-depth, related tasks combined to create a project, exhibit, or demonstration. In contrast to multiple-choice, matching, or true/false formats, which are scored objectively, performance assessment requires interpretation of student work. The introduction of a rubric or scoring guide, with carefully defined criteria connected to standards, helps teachers reach consistency in the interpretation of assessment data.

Performance assessment, although generally confined to the classroom, can occur on a large-scale basis. The features of performance assessment include the following:

- Topics of high interest that are thought provoking and encourage exploration
- Key principles, concepts, and "big ideas"
- Vocabulary and language patterns associated with a theme or topic
- Higher-level thinking and processing
- Multiple avenues, which often rely on multiple resources, to reach conclusions or solutions
- Questions that lead to related issues or new ideas

Student self-assessment is also a valuable data source that is part of classroom performance. Chapter 7 elaborates on different types of **self-** and **peer assessment** within the classroom routine. Figure 6.1 illustrates the relationship between the components of performance assessment for English language learners. It shows how performance assessment is grounded in standards and embedded in curriculum and instruction.

Figure 6.1 A Model of Standards-Based Performance Assessment for English Language Learners

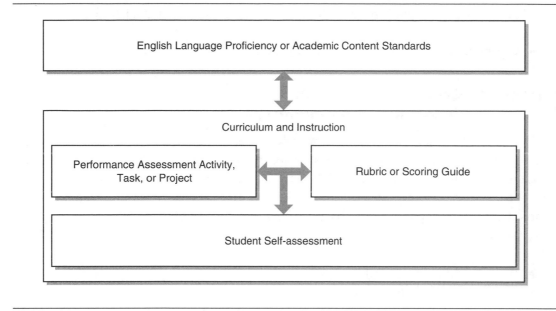

THE IMPORTANCE OF PERFORMANCE ASSESSMENT FOR ENGLISH LANGUAGE LEARNERS

Large-scale assessment assumes a central role in standards-based reform. If performance-based, **classroom assessment** is to be given any weight within an accountability system, it must consist of sets of standard tasks, administered under standard conditions, and analyzed in standard ways. Professional development must be afforded teachers in designing and piloting performance assessments as well as agreeing in the interpretation of student work.

There is tremendous variability from teacher to teacher that affects student performance. **Reliability**, or consistency, in planning, implementing, and scoring student performances contributes to valid assessment. As a result, teachers and other stakeholders can have confidence in the results and data can be aggregated, or combined, across classrooms, grade levels, departments, schools, districts, or states. Only then can classroom assessment complement or augment other large-scale efforts.

Performance assessment has been recognized as a viable approach at the classroom and large-scale levels (Darling-Hammond, Ancess, & Falk, 1995; Glatthorn, 1998; Guskey, 1994; Smith, Smith, & De Lisi, 2001). One of the hallmarks of performance assessment is its authenticity with roots in real-life experiences. According to Wiggins (1993), authenticity not only carries face **validity** but is of value in and of itself. For English language learners, planning authentic performance-based assessment entails the following:

- Use of natural language geared to the students' levels of language proficiency
- Tasks or projects that represent real-world experiences
- Tasks and projects that are complex, contextualized, and visually or graphically supported
- Connections between the tasks and the students' lives and cultures

Factors to Consider in the Design of Performance Assessment

Classrooms, schools, districts, and states need to identify the factors that affect student performance. English language learners are an extremely heterogeneous population in terms of their linguistic and cultural backgrounds as well as in the types and continuity of their educational experiences. These student-level considerations, listed below, provide the backdrop for the design of curriculum, instruction, and assessment.

- Age, grade level, or both
- Level(s) of English language proficiency
- Academic achievement in English or **native language**
- Educational history
- Familiarity with working with partners or in small groups
- Familiarity with project or inquiry-based learning

Besides these student variables, there are also teacher considerations in planning performance assessment. The amount of time teachers have to work with English language learners determines whether the performance consists of short-term activities or more long-term tasks or projects. Resources, such as the integration of technology, and the amount of necessary support also affect how performance assessment is designed. Potential collaboration with teachers is another part of the planning phase. Before embarking on performance assessment for their English language learners, teachers need to think about these factors:

- Allocation of time
- Medium of instruction (English, native language, or both)
- Available resources
- Grouping of students
- Amount of visual, graphic, and linguistic support
- Collaboration with other teachers or family members.

THE ROLE OF RUBRICS IN PERFORMANCE ASSESSMENT

What differentiates instruction from assessment in a performance-based model is the use of rubrics for documentation and interpretation of student work. Instructional assessment assumes that instruction and assessment are interwoven, mirror images of each other. The fact that assessment is embedded in instruction, rather than its by-product, creates a clear **alignment** between the two and allows for a seamless transition from one to the other.

Rubrics, or scoring guides, are a recognized resource for elementary and secondary teachers across the content areas (Farr & Tone, 1994; Hein & Price, 1994; Taggart, Phifer, Nixon, & Wood, 1998, to name a few). Rubrics are equally important in the instruction and assessment of English language learners (Farr & Trumbell, 1997; Genesee & Upshur, 1996; Gottlieb, 1999a; Navarrete & Gustke, 1996; O'Malley & Pierce, 1996). By delineating clear-cut criteria, rubrics describe the goals for learning and identify the extent to which students have met them.

Uses for Rubrics

Besides serving as the basis for establishing agreement among teachers for performance tasks, rubrics have numerous useful applications. Standards-based rubrics, as expressions of performance assessment, are the primary source of evidence and documentation of teaching and learning. Rubrics, whether adopted, adapted, or created, can do the following:

- Offer a uniform set of criteria or descriptors for anchoring student, teacher, or scorer judgment of student work
- Identify a target or benchmark to be reached by students and the requisite stepping stones to accomplishing it
- Demystify assessment for students and parents through a shared set of expectations
- Establish a uniform process for teachers to analyze and interpret student samples
- Serve as a means for translating standards into practice
- Offer a focus for instruction and assessment
- Become a basis for collaboration and coordination among teachers
- Promote articulation and continuity for teachers from one grade to the next
- Spur opportunities for consensus building among teachers
- Provide an organizing framework for recording and reporting results

Although there are many benefits of rubrics use, there is also potential for their overuse or abuse. If rubrics become a de facto expression of standards and curriculum, teachers may make erroneous assumptions about what their students can actually do. Also, if rubrics identify the criteria by which student work is to be interpreted, then in essence, they can impose limitations on the range of acceptable student behaviors. Table 6.1 gives point and counterpoint in regard to rubric use.

For English language learners, rubrics have applicability to the measurement of **language proficiency** and **academic achievement**. For language proficiency, rubrics delineate the developmental pathways that represent the **second language acquisition** continuum. In contrast, rubrics designed to measure academic achievement describe the absolute performance of students in relation to academic content. Unlike language proficiency rubrics where reaching the standards is generally the

Table 6.1 The Uses and Abuses of Rubrics

Uses	Abuses
• Aligned with standards	• Restricted by standards
• Descriptive of what an assigned numeral means	• Constructed as an arbiter of quality
• Basis for consensus building	• Constricted in range of accepted variability
• Focused on instruction and assessment	• Prescriptive of instruction and assessment
• Uniform analysis and interpretation of student work	• Agent of control

end point, the **designations** or levels in rubrics for academic achievement generally extend beyond students "meeting" to those "exceeding" standards. To be equitable, these rubrics should acknowledge English language learners' levels of English or native language proficiency within their descriptors (as outlined in the reflection).

REFLECTION: Modifying Rubrics for English Language Learners

Look for rubrics that have been designed for **proficient English students**. Think of ways you might modify them to better meet the needs of English language learners. Perhaps you may add descriptors or proficiency levels. Perhaps you may need to add visual or graphic support. Perhaps you may weigh the criteria differently or add another component descriptive of second language learners. Perhaps you may need to make provision for the students' native language. Share your ideas with other teachers at the same grade level.

Types and Purposes of Rubrics

There are a variety of rubric types, each of which corresponds to a particular form of student performance. The selection of a rubric should parallel how instructional assessment is delivered. Rubrics offer options for teachers for data collection and interpretation. Activities or tasks of short duration lend themselves to **checklists** or **rating scales.** Longer tasks and projects, associated with more extensive and in-depth instruction, are better served by more comprehensive rubrics as in analytic or holistic scales. A spectrum of rubric types is presented as a continuum in Figure 6.2.

In planning instructional assessment, the form of student responses must be compatible with the type of rubric teachers select to interpret the data. In addition, the rubric should reflect how the standards, represented in the classroom by language and content objectives, are assessed. In that way, there is a strong connection between instruction and assessment.

Figure 6.2 Types of Rubrics From Discrete to Holistic Scales

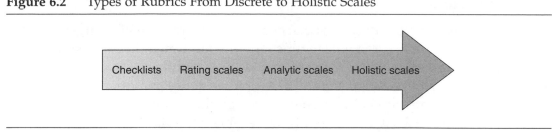

SOURCE: Adapted from Gottlieb (2004a).

Checklists

Checklists are dichotomous scales (having two options) in which identified skills, competencies, strategies, or **language functions** are marked as either present or absent. On the plus side is their ease of use; therefore, they may be appropriate for students, parents, and teachers. On the downside, checklists lack substantive information; they do not provide detailed descriptions of the range of quality needed to assess more complex performances (Arter & McTighe, 2001).

English language learners may not be familiar with performance assessment; in addition, their language proficiency may preclude them from expressing themselves in English or creating substantive products, if directions are given only in English. Therefore, checklists become an entrée into their involvement in the assessment process. Table 6.2 is an example of a checklist that relies on "yes" or "no" responses to document English language learners' use of math strategies.

Table 6.2 Self-Assessment Checklist of Math Strategies for English Language Learners

What do you do to solve math problems? Put an X in the box to answer YES or NO.

	YES	NO
1. I use my first language to help me.		
2. I draw pictures to help me.		
3. I use things in my classroom (objects) to help me.		
4. I ask my friends to help me.		
5. I look for examples in the book.		
6. I read the problems aloud.		
7. I ask the teacher questions.		
8. I try to picture the problem when I do mental math.		
9. I use oral directions, not written directions.		
10. I check what I have done.		

Rating Scales

Rating scales are types of rubrics that express the degree to which targeted skills, competencies, strategies, or language functions are performed. In contrast to checklists, rating scales have either a range of frequency—as in *always, sometimes, never*—or quality—as in *great, good,* or *awful.* These options define the extent to which the identified competency or skill is present; although there is more descriptive information than in a checklist, it may not be as reliable. English language learners can begin to extend their repertoire of rubric use by responding to a rating scale that has been expanded from a checklist, first using one with three choices and then later, one with four.

An example of a rating scale is a needs assessment survey. The one in Table 6.3 is designed for student self-assessment and offers insight into their interests, motivation, and experiences as well as useful information for curriculum and lesson planning. It is a four-point rating scale of English language learners' estimates of their English language use across **language domains**; this one rates the students' listening comprehension (Gottlieb, 1999a).

Table 6.3   Listening Self-Assessment Rating Scale for English Language Learners

Think about all the times you listen to English. Put an X in the box that says how well you understand what is said, from *Not Well* to *Great!*

When LISTENING to English, I understand	Not Well	OK	Quite Well	Great!
1. Questions that ask who, what, where, or when				
2. Music (such as hip-hop or rap)				
3. Programs and news on TV				
4. Information on the radio				
5. Announcements at school				
6. What people say on the telephone				
7. What teachers say in class				
8. Oral reports my classmates give				
9. The main idea when someone reads aloud				
10. Jokes my classmates tell				

Analytic Scales

Analytic scales, generally expressed in the form of a matrix, are a type of rubric that delineates specific dimensions or traits of the construct being measured (such as listening comprehension). For English language learners, the criteria associated with each dimension of English language proficiency correspond to components of second-language development. These criteria or descriptors are usually presented developmentally in a series of four to six performance levels.

This rubric is the most diagnostic in nature because it gives information regarding what students can do along each dimension and language proficiency or performance level which, when combined, yields a student profile. In this way, analytic scales may be closely tied to instruction and relate to students the most important aspects of language or content learning. However, it is the most complex of all rubric types; there is needed time to score student work, and often, professional development is required for teachers to use it with ease and reliability. Table 6.4 outlines the benefits and challenges of analytic scales.

The criteria or descriptors in analytic scales should represent what students can do at each of the designated levels of language proficiency or academic performance. As such, they need to be clearly stated, observable, and assessable behaviors. Table 6.5 is an example of an analytic scale for documenting listening comprehension of English language learners. The language domain of listening, in this instance, consists of four dimensions, with two criteria for the four language proficiency levels.

Table 6.4   Advantages and Disadvantages of Using Analytic Scales

Advantages	Disadvantages
• Criteria or descriptors match specified dimensions or components.	• Decisions regarding which dimensions to measure are challenging.
• Differential growth patterns emerge according to dimensions.	• They are rather time-consuming to score.
• A student profile informs instruction.	• Reaching consensus on scoring is difficult.
• Diagnostic information becomes available from the multiple dimensions of the scale.	• It is assumed that each dimension of the rubric is of equal weight.

Holistic Scales

Holistic scales of language proficiency or academic achievement are a type of rubric that provides an overall description of student competencies by level of performance. Several criteria or descriptors are presented along a developmental continuum from least to most proficient.

At a classroom level, assignment to a language proficiency or academic achievement level can be based on accumulated evidence gathered over time from a variety of activities, tasks, and projects. Individual, paired, or small-group instructional

Table 6.5 A Sample Analytic Scale for Documenting Listening Comprehension of English Language Learners

	Proficiency Level			
	1. Beginner	2. Intermediate	3. Advanced	4. Expert
1. Understanding of spoken language	• Understand short utterances of social language • Begin to comprehend with graphic or visual support	• Understand social language • Comprehend with graphic or visual support	• Understand social and general academic language • Comprehend without reliance on support	• Fully understand social and specialized academic language • Comprehend on par with proficient peers
2. Response to oral directions	• Follow one-step oral commands • Respond (nonverbally) to requests by peers	• Follow multiple-step oral directions • Respond (nonverbally) to teachers or school announcements	• Follow multiple-step instructions embedded in extended discourse • Respond (nonverbally) to discourse from unfamiliar speakers	• Follow complex instructions similar to proficient peers • Respond (nonverbally) to discourse from CDs, computer programs, or cassettes
3. Use of strategies	• Associate sounds and words with meaning, with presence of visual support • Use manipulatives or real-life materials to illustrate oral statements	• Focus on key words of the utterance with visual and context cues • Use manipulatives or draw pictures to illustrate a series of directions	• Develop listening strategies with less reliance on visual or context cues • Use visually supported charts, graphs, or tables to compare oral information	• Use listening strategies with and without support • Complete charts, graphs, or tables to show comparisons given orally
4. Overall listening comprehension	• Begin to show explicit comprehension when visual support is present • Respond (nonverbally) to oral commands, statements, or social courtesies	• Demonstrate explicit comprehension when visual support is present • Respond (nonverbally) to multiple-step oral directions and instructions	• Begin to demonstrate implicit comprehension when visual or graphic support is present • Respond (nonverbally) to oral discourse	• Demonstrate implicit comprehension comparable to proficient peers • Respond (nonverbally) to oral discourse with figurative language

Table 6.6   Advantages and Disadvantages of Using Holistic Scales

Advantages	Disadvantages
• Overall, global indicator of student performance	• A one-dimensional scale with little diagnostic information
• Easy to score against student exemplars	• Summary scores can be mistakenly confused with grades
• Results readily communicated to general education teachers and parents	• Broad intervals between levels; lack of precision of measurement
• Applicable across many tasks, contexts, and settings	• Need to use in combination with other types of assessment information

assessment within the classroom may contribute to the students' ratings. For large-scale assessment, holistic scales are used to describe individual student performance at one point in time.

The number-one consideration in selecting any rubric is its match with the purpose for assessment. As with any rubric or scale, there are pros and cons attached to its use. Holistic scales are beneficial in providing a summary score that is easily communicated to a variety of stakeholders. On the negative side, no one score should ever be the sole basis of decision making. Table 6.6 balances the advantages and disadvantages of using holistic scales.

Holistic scales can be created from analytic ones; instead of having individual dimensions, all criteria are combined in determining a performance level. Table 6.7 is an example of a holistic scale or rubric for listening comprehension with a single set of criteria converted from the analytic one presented in Table 6.5. It may be applied to English language learners who are acquiring English or proficient English speakers who are being instructed in another language, such as in dual-language or foreign language settings. As a global indicator of listening comprehension, the rubric provides summary information to teachers for each proficiency level.

With a choice of different types of rubrics, teachers may struggle in determining which one is most appropriate for a given instructional assessment activity, task, or project. English language learners' proficiency levels are one deciding factor; how the information is best reported and used is another. The reflection in Appendix 6.1 is aimed at having teachers match examples of instructional assessment geared to classrooms with the various kinds of rubrics. There is a caveat, however, in that although it is possible that more than one type of rubric could be used, only the most typical one is marked in Appendix 6.2.

Task-Specific Scales

Analytic and holistic rubrics or scales are developmental and represent more complex learning than checklists or rating scales. Developmental rubrics are defined by a set of criteria that scaffold, or build on each other, from one performance level

Table 6.7   A Sample Holistic Scale for Listening Comprehension

Proficiency Level			
1. Beginner	*2. Intermediate*	*3. Advanced*	*4. Expert*
• Understand short utterances of social language	• Understand social language	• Understand social and general academic language	• Fully understand social and specialized academic language
• Follow one-step oral commands	• Follow multiple-step oral directions	• Follow a series of multiple-step oral instructions	• Follow oral instructions similar to proficient peers
• Associate sounds and words with meaning, with presence of visual support	• Focus on key words of the utterance with visual and context cues	• Develop listening strategies with less reliance on visual or context cues	• Use listening strategies with and without support
• Begin to show explicit comprehension when visual support is present	• Demonstrate explicit comprehension when visual support is present	• Begin to demonstrate implicit comprehension when visual or graphic support is present	• Demonstrate implicit comprehension comparable to proficient peers

to the next to form a logical progression or sequence. The criteria are broad enough to apply to an array of instructional assessment approaches, tasks, or projects either in the classroom or in large-scale settings. At times, however, these scales can be converted to ones for specific tasks or projects. Figure 6.3 shows the relationships between these different types of developmental rubrics.

Figure 6.3   Types of Developmental Rubrics

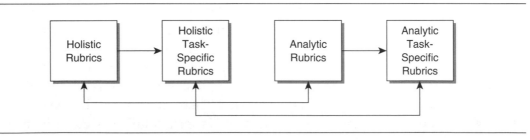

Task-specific rubrics, whether holistic or analytic, are crafted for a single use, from either a **constructed response** item on a large-scale assessment or a classroom project. At the classroom level, these scales are geared to help students organize their work, inform parents of long-term assignments, and allow teachers to plan instruction and assessment. The downside to task-specific rubrics is that they may be

Table 6.8   Advantages and Disadvantages of Task-Specific Rubrics

Advantages	Disadvantages
• Concrete feedback to students and parents	• Not generalizable due to their discrete nature
• Direct link to instruction	• Narrow in application
• Map of specified components of tasks or projects	• Limited usefulness outside of identified tasks or projects
• Ease of scoring against specified criteria	• Too often equated with grading practices

time-consuming to create. Table 6.8 offers pros and cons of using task-specific rubrics.

It is advisable for teachers to use developmental holistic or analytic rubrics as templates for designing task-specific ones. In this way, there is continuity in terms of assigning performance levels; this consistency contributes to reliability in scoring over time. In addition, students who have gained familiarity with one form of a rubric can readily see its relationship to the other.

Tables 6.9 and 6.10 are illustrative examples of how a holistic, developmental scale can be translated into a task-specific one. In both cases, there are four performance levels (from 1 to 4) with parallel criteria. However, the task-specific rubric (in Table 6.10) lays out specific descriptors by which middle or high students are to be evaluated on a standards-based project about managing a budget (described in Appendix 6.3).

OVERALL FEATURES OF RUBRICS

Student work produced by performance assessment is often interpreted by teachers' use of rubrics or scoring guides. Standards-based criteria or descriptors in rubrics, reflective of instruction, aid in informing teaching. In addition, they offer a uniform way for teachers to reliably assign a score or designation, such as a language proficiency level. Appendix 6.4 is a checklist of the features that should be present in rubrics designed for English language learners.

SUMMARY AND FINAL THOUGHTS

Increasingly, classrooms, schools, school districts, and states are complementing traditional testing methods with performance assessment to have evidence of student performance on **multiple measures**. Having students produce original work around major themes, ideas, or issues encourages deep learning and **supports** in-depth teaching. Incorporating higher-order thinking into performance tasks encountered in the "real world" enables students to develop and demonstrate

Table 6.9   A Sample Holistic Rubric for Student Projects

Level 4: Champion

- Develop and implement a comprehensive action plan
- Rely on materials and resources to formulate and express ideas
- Collect appropriate amounts and kinds of information
- Use visual and graphic representation to support ideas
- Systematically analyze and interpret information
- Use evidence from analysis to make and justify decisions

Level 3: Contender

- Develop and implement an action plan based on project descriptor
- Use materials and resources to develop ideas
- Collect relevant, but still incomplete, information
- Present logical ideas through visual and graphic representation
- Analyze and interpret some information
- Use evidence from analysis to make decisions

Level 2: Competitor

- Follow a given action plan or project descriptor
- Use some materials and resources related to the theme or project
- Collect some information related to the theme or project
- Express ideas through visual and/or graphic representation
- Attempt to analyze and interpret information
- Use some evidence to make decisions

Level 1: Challenger

- Attempt to follow a project descriptor
- Use some materials and/or resources
- Collect nonrelated or little information
- Include some visual and/or graphic representation
- Lack analyses and interpretation of information
- Make decisions without evidence

SOURCE: Adapted from Gottlieb (1999b).

abilities to use in school and life (Darling-Hammond et al., 1995). Using performance assessment at a large-scale level produces accountability for learning that is more authentic and reflective of the mission of schools (Neill, Guisbond, & Schaeffer, 2004).

English language learners profit from performance assessment because it can readily be differentiated to meet their linguistic, cultural, and educational needs. Language and content targets, grounded in standards, are the starting point. Rubrics serve as the bridge between instruction and assessment.

Table 6.10   Conversion of a Holistic Rubric Into a Holistic, Task-Specific Rubric for the Project "Managing a Budget"

Level 4: Champion

- Develop and implement a comprehensive plan for spending and saving money
- Use newspapers, magazines, and technology to support budget decisions
- Fill out bank slips, maintain a journal, and determine money saved and spent
- Construct a graph that accurately displays weekly budget and supports oral report
- Systematically analyze and interpret information pertaining to managing a budget
- Explain effectiveness in keeping a budget in an oral report along with a graphic display of work

Level 3: Contender

- Develop and implement a plan for spending and saving money based on the project descriptor
- Use newspapers, magazines, and technology to determine prices
- Consistently fill out bank slips, maintain a journal, and determine money saved and spent
- Construct a graph that presents logical information
- Analyze and interpret some budgetary information
- Describe how to manage a budget in an oral report along with an organized graphic display of work

Level 2: Competitor

- Engage in student self-assessment based on the project descriptor
- Use some relevant resources, such as newspapers and magazines
- Sporadically fill out bank slips, make journal entries, and determine finances
- Express the idea of a budget through a graph
- Attempt to analyze and interpret information related to a budget
- Give an oral report related to display of some written and graphic information

Level 1: Challenger

- Attempt student self-assessment from the project descriptor
- Use some related materials and/or resources
- Provide little information from bank slips and journal entries
- Include some pictures and may produce a graph
- Present information as facts without analyses or interpretation
- Give oral report with sparse written or graphic evidence

APPENDIX 6.1

REFLECTION: Matching Instruction to Assessment

Think about the classroom activities, tasks, and projects for your English language learners. Which rubric is most appropriate for the student performance described? Mark the corresponding box on the right. Share some examples of how you match instruction with specific types of rubrics with your colleagues.

	Checklist	Rating Scale	Analytic Scale	Holistic Scale
1. Responding to oral commands				
2. Producing a process-writing piece				
3. Demonstrating a procedure				
4. Completing a satisfaction survey				
5. Designing a brochure				
6. Writing a paragraph or two				
7. Developing and conducting research; then analyzing and reporting results				
8. Creating a poetry portfolio				
9. Formulating and answering yes/no questions				

APPENDIX 6.2

REFLECTION: Possible Types of Rubrics for Matching Instruction to Assessment

	Checklist	Rating Scale	Analytic Scale	Holistic Scale
1. Responding to oral commands	x			
2. Producing a process-writing piece			x	
3. Demonstrating a procedure				x
4. Completing a satisfaction survey		x		
5. Designing a brochure			x	
6. Writing a paragraph or two				x
7. Developing and conducting research; then analyzing and reporting results			x	
8. Creating a poetry portfolio			x	
9. Formulating and answering yes/no questions	x			

APPENDIX 6.3

An Interdisciplinary Project for Middle School English Language Learners: "Managing the Budget"

This project is designed for students who perhaps have had limited formal schooling, may be new to the United States, or whose English language proficiency is at the beginning to midrange stages. It is intended to cross content area boundaries and begs collaboration with teachers who work with these students on a daily basis. Multiple types of assessment data are used to determine the students' language proficiency and academic achievement.

Standards

Academic Content Standards:

Math: Statistics and probability

Performance Standards: Work with data in the context of real-world situations

Social studies: Economics—Describe and explain the role of money, banking, and savings in everyday life

Media and technology: Use computers to acquire, organize, analyze, and communicate information

English Language Proficiency Standards (taken from World-class Instructional Design and Assessment Consortium, 2004):

Social and instructional language: Identify, match, categorize, analyze, and evaluate resources needed to complete assignments

Language of language arts: Produce words, phrases, notes, charts, paragraphs to convey information

Language of math: Match vocabulary, classify examples, and order steps of procedures involved in problem solving

Language of social studies: Chart trends and compare data based on statements from texts and charts

Background for Instructional Assessment

Instructional assessment ideas: Economics plays an important role in personal, family, and business life. To become responsible contributors to our society, we need to be able to organize and manage our resources.

Resources and materials: Bank forms, computer spreadsheet, newspapers, calculators, graphic organizers

Instructional assessment products: A display with pictures and graphs (exhibition) and an oral report (demonstration)

(Continued)

Duration of project: Approximately one week

Content Objectives:

- Math: Calculate and average expenses; chart results to detect trend data
- Social studies: Discuss role of economics in everyday life based on analysis of data
- Media and technology: Use calculators, produce spreadsheets, design accurate pie graphs

Language Objectives:

- Social and instructional language: Identify, match, categorize, analyze, and evaluate information from newspapers and magazines to complete assignments
- Language of language arts: Produce words, phrases, notes, charts, paragraphs to convey information on a poster, maintain a journal, and give an oral report
- Language of math: Match vocabulary, classify examples, and order steps of procedures involved in keeping track of expenses
- Language of social studies: Chart daily expenses and compare data based on pie graphs or spread sheets

Sample Performance Tasks and Activities

Task 1: A Poster Display. Given a fixed budget, have students (in pairs) decide how much money should be spent and saved. Students can set a goal to buy food for their family, for example, or purchase items to set up a business. All money not spent is to be put into a bank account. The allocation of money (total amount or subdivided, for example, by categories of expenses) is to be represented in a bar graph that is to be incorporated into a poster display.

As part of this task, have students do the following:

Activity 1: Look at newspapers or magazines, cut out pictures, and list potential purchases and their prices. Using a graphic organizer, categorize types of purchases.

Activity 2: Determine the money spent by using a calculator or creating a spread sheet. Subtract the total amount spent from the budgeted amount.

Activity 3: Make a pie or bar graph (with a computer) that shows the total amount spent in relation to the budgeted amount.

Activity 4: Practice filling out deposit slips from a bank and/or visit a bank to see what kinds of services are available. Make a deposit slip for the amount of money saved.

Activity 5: Produce a poster about managing their budget with all relevant information collected and analyzed for the project, such as graphs, pictures, and deposit slips.

Task 2: An Oral Report. Students are to present the information they have collected, analyzed, and displayed. As part of the report, students will evaluate how well they managed a budget.

As part of this task, have students do the following:

Activity 1: Maintain a process journal (photo, oral, or written) during the project and record each phase of the project.

Activity 2: Use new vocabulary associated with the math and social studies concepts of the unit with a partner. Match vocabulary with their pictures and graph on their display.

Activity 3: Complete a graphic organizer with the relevant information that can be used for the report.

Activity 4: Practice giving an oral report with their partner about the steps in managing a budget. Evaluate how effective they were in managing a budget.

Types of Classroom Assessment

- Create a checklist from the activities so the students will be aware of the short-term goals of the project and the teacher can provide ongoing feedback. Have students review the checklist with their partners.
- Have students maintain a journal of their daily activities. Teachers may provide feedback to the journal entries.
- Select and share with students an oral language rubric that reflects what is to be assessed in the oral report.
- Use the project rubric (see Table 6.10), a four-point holistic scale, to assess the overall performance of the students on the project. Reference it back to the academic content and language proficiency standards as well as to the content and language objectives.

SOURCE: Adapted from Gottlieb (2000).

APPENDIX 6.4

A Checklist of Rubric Features for English Language Learners

Does the rubric	YES	NO
1. Reflect what the students can do at varying levels of English language proficiency?		
2. Document observable student performance?		
3. Represent the activity, task, or project being assessed?		
4. Match standards, instruction, and assessment?		
5. Appear teacher, student, or parent friendly, depending on its audience?		
6. Allow students to express themselves in multiple ways?		
7. Lend itself for use in multiple contexts?		
8. Provide teachers clear-cut criteria to analyze student work?		
9. Promote articulation from teacher to teacher?		
10. Relate meaningful descriptors of teaching and learning?		

SOURCE: Adapted from Short et al. (2000).

Supports for Student, Classroom, and Large-Scale Assessment

The Bridge to Student Understanding

Children are the bridge to heaven.

—A Persian proverb

A primary goal of **English as a second language** or bilingual services for **English language learners** is to facilitate students' acquisition of English and academic content on their road to reaching parity with their English proficient peers. Support for English language proficiency obviously proceeds in the students' second language, whereas that for **academic achievement** can occur in their **native language**, second language, or both. This chapter describes three major categories of support that are useful in the instruction and **assessment** of English language learners: (1) visual and graphic representation, (2) instructional techniques, and (3) student reflection. Together, these **supports** promote and reinforce language and content learning.

USE OF VISUAL OR GRAPHIC SUPPORT

Visual or graphic support is a mainstay of the instructional repertoire of teachers working with English language learners. There are innumerable reasons for teachers to incorporate pictures, diagrams, photographs, tables, charts, graphs, authentic materials, **manipulatives**, multimedia, and graphic organizers into the instructional assessment cycle. These supports provide English language learners with the following:

- Multiple avenues for accessing content, constructing meaning, and communicating ideas
- Various means of demonstrating understanding of academic concepts that are not language dependent
- Comprehensible input for processing language
- Opportunities to be active participants in hands-on learning
- Tools for engaging in higher-order thinking
- Tools for organizing and integrating language and content
- Validation or confirmation of what they know and are able to do

The next sections offer ideas on how different forms of visual and graphic support can aid in the instructional assessment of English language learners.

Graphic Organizers

Graphic organizers and visual frameworks are powerful instructional assessment tools for all students (Ewy, 2002; Hyerle, 1996). They are particularly useful for English language learners whose English language proficiency precludes them from expressing their conceptual knowledge through language (when it is English). Rather than being faced with producing an in-class essay, for example, graphic organizers invite English language learners to communicate the same key ideas in less intimidating, less language-driven, and more relevant ways.

Table 7.1 shows five common types of graphic organizers that can be used in the core content areas with all students and in particular, with English language learners. The format of each organizer encourages students to engage in higher-level thinking with minimal dependence on literacy. While graphic organizers may be the first step in a multiphased writing process for **proficient English students**, they may be the end point for English language learners who may only be able to express themselves in English using words, phrases, or short sentences.

Some techniques implicit in the instruction of graphic organizers are helpful for English language learners of all ages; however, how they are used needs to be explicitly taught. The notion of comparison and contrast, illustrated with Venn diagrams,

Table 7.1 Examples of Use of Graphic Organizers Across the Core Content Areas

	Language Arts	Mathematics	Science	Social Studies
Venn diagrams: Comparing and contrasting two entities	• Two characters • Two settings • Two genres	• Two operations • Two geometric figures • Two forms of proportion	• Two body systems or organs • Two animals or plants • Two forms of matter	• Two conflicts • Two forms of government • Two forms of transportation
T-charts: Sorting or categorizing objects or concepts	• Main idea/details • Facts/opinions • Differing points of view • Pros/cons	• Area/perimeter • Fractions/decimals • Addition/subtraction	• Forms of energy • Senses • Vertebrates/invertebrates	• Types of transportation • Types of habitats • Features of cities, states, or regions
Cycles: Producing a series of connected events or a process	• Plot lines in stories or pieces of literature • Life cycles in biographies or autobiographies	• Steps in problem solving • Collecting, analyzing, and reporting data	• Scientific inquiry • Life cycles of organisms • Water cycle	• Conflict/resolution • Elections in a democracy
Cause and effect: Outlining a relationship	• Responses of characters to events or situations	• Solving algebraic equations • Geometric theorems	• Chemical reactions • Adaptation • Weather events	• Political movements • Economic trends
Semantic webs: Connecting themes with categories	• Root words and affixes • Multiple meaning of words and phrases	• Types and features of polygons • Types and characteristics of angles	• Foods and their nutritional ingredients • Types and characteristics of rocks	• Types of human and civil rights • Impact of economic policies on governments or nations

may be the entry point for English language learners for working with multiple sources of information. Beginners may start with analyzing the physical attributes of two objects, figures, or characters. Even young children can complete this type of graphic, with assistance, based on pictures or observation, such as comparing butterflies and moths, cars and trucks, squares and triangles.

T-charts are another type of graphic organizer applicable across content areas. English language learners may follow a set of teacher directions that include examples of math, science, or social studies concepts and then classify pictures or pictures with words into relevant groups. For assessment, students may engage in either (1) an open sort with the pictures or pictures with words, using the T-chart, where they themselves define the categories, or (2) a closed sort, where the groups are assigned. Examples of concepts that lend themselves to this type of graphic organizer include objects that sink or float, resources of China or Japan, and acute or obtuse angles.

To illustrate a cycle, beginning English language learners need only to draw pictures, produce labels, or match terms associated with each phase. As they acquire English, the students can then be expected to describe each stage, orally or in writing. To demonstrate their understanding of cause and effect, English language learners can show the relations between actions and reactions between characters, or the antecedents and effects of major historical events. Finally, the use of semantic webs stimulates vocabulary development and lets students visualize how to organize categories representative of themes, concepts, or big ideas from personal experiences or academic content.

Graphic Organizers and English Language Patterns

Specific language patterns in English are associated with each type of graphic organizer. In acquiring **academic language proficiency**, English language learners must be able to reproduce key words and phrases that mark the relationships depicted in the organizer. Because of age and developmental differences, the markers we use in English are often different for younger and older students. Table 7.2 delineates some language patterns that trigger higher-level thinking when using graphic organizers with younger and older students.

Graphic organizers play an important role in the instructional assessment of English language learners. However, to be effective, these graphic representations must convey meaning so that English language learners can access content. As with all sound instruction, teachers have to model and reinforce the procedures, the processes, and examples of their use. Until students are totally familiar with and have practiced each format, graphic organizers should not be considered for assessment. Appendix 7.1 is a **checklist** of the features that should be present in graphic organizers designed for instruction and assessment of English language learners.

Charts, Graphs, and Tables

Charts, graphs, and tables are likely companions to expository text in the content areas of mathematics, science, and social studies. Through these graphic representations, English language learners can decipher relationships with minimal dependence on print. Information generally related to academic achievement is presented in a condensed and organized format to allow students to engage in analysis as they

Table 7.2   Key Words and Phrases Associated With the Use of Graphic Organizers
With Younger and Older Students

Type of Graphic Organizer	Language Patterns for Younger Students	Language Patterns for Older Students
Venn diagrams	Both . . . Just like . . . The two . . . . . . and One has . . . but the other doesn't. Not as . . . (adj) as . . . Less/more (adj) than . . .	Similar/identical to . . . Neither . . . nor Likewise . . . On the other hand . . . However . . . In contrast . . .
T-charts	These . . . those	This set . . . that set
Cycles	Before . . . after First, second, last To start (begin) . . . at the end	Initially . . . subsequently In the first place . . . followed by . . . concluded with
Cause and effect	When . . . then . . . If . . . then Since . . . Because . . .	Without . . . won't (can't) Unless . . . perhaps (surely) When . . . it causes As a result . . . therefore Consequently . . .
Semantic webs	These are all . . . These are different ways . . . The main idea is	There are connections among The categories include . . . These groups are linked to . . .

formulate their ideas. Through charts and graphs, English language learners not only learn how to sort information but simultaneously acquire the language of categorization as well.

For Academic Achievement

Charts and tables display information in a linear fashion, either vertically or horizontally (such as in bar graphs or histograms). Pie charts tend to express the distribution of information in terms of percentages within a circle. Information in these graphic supports can be in the form of line art, numerals, symbols, or text. Table 7.3 illustrates the application of different types of graphic support to the content areas of science, social studies, mathematics, and language arts.

For Language Proficiency

Language proficiency comes into play when students transform information on tables, charts, or graphs into speech or writing. For tables and charts, English

Table 7.3   Examples of Uses of Charts or Tables, Bar Graphs or Histograms, and Pie Charts Across the Content Areas

Content Area/Strand	Chart or Table	Bar Graphs or Histograms	Pie Charts (in %)
Science–Astronomy	Missions to explore planets, types of vehicles, dates	Miles of planets from sun (with number of days per year)	Atmospheric compositions of planets
Social studies–Regions	Major U.S. cities, year founded, locations	Population change of cities or states over decades	Ethnic composition of communities
Mathematics–Real-life problem solving	Types of weekend activities, by day, description	Log of weekend activities over a month (in hours)	Time devoted to each activity over the month
Language arts-Strategies	Types of reading strategies, uses, personal response	Times used per assignment, book, or unit	Usefulness of each reading strategy

language learners can either read the information horizontally, in rows, or vertically, by columns. Depending on the language proficiency levels of the students, pairs of rows or columns can be used for comparison or contrast, or an entire set of information can be the basis for analysis.

Students themselves can be encouraged to fill in charts, following the patterns modeled in completed cells. English language learners can then be prompted to ask each other questions such as these regarding the information the chart contains: "Which planet is farthest from the sun?" "Which city has the most people?" "Which activities do you do on Saturdays?" "Which reading strategy is used the least?" Teachers can then model additional language patterns to extend the students' oral responses.

When converting information on a graphic to connected discourse, as in creating a written paragraph, students need to understand the use of linking words so that the language will flow and be cohesive. More sophisticated and proficient writers may show the connections through words such as *however, but,* and *while* as well as present information through subordinate clauses. Thus the use of charts, graphs, and tables aids in students' development of thinking processes, academic achievement, and language proficiency.

CROSS-CUTTING INSTRUCTIONAL ASSESSMENT TECHNIQUES

In this section, we explore how effective instructional supports enhance student learning across the content areas. If these techniques are taught explicitly, English language learners should have greater access to challenging curriculum and will be able to deal more effectively with language and content demands of the classroom.

Teacher Input

The usefulness of visual or graphic support for English language learners in acquiring and expressing the language and content of the curriculum is quite transparent. Other teaching techniques apply across language arts, mathematics, science, and social studies to support instructional assessment with or without graphic support. Those highlighted in this chapter, as throughout the book, include helping English language learners with the following:

- Acquiring and using learning strategies
- Interacting with partners or in small groups
- Making cultural and experiential connections
- Engaging in higher-level thinking
- Reflecting on their learning
- Being actively involved in learning

Acquisition and Use of Learning Strategies

Learning strategies for English language learners are geared to enhance the acquisition of oral language and literacy, increase test-taking skills, improve cognition, raise metacognitive awareness, and promote social/affective effectiveness (O'Malley & Chamot, 1990). A sizeable portion of TESOL's (Teachers of English to Speakers of Other Languages) 1997 pre-K–12 ESL standards are devoted to strategic teaching and learning—as in "Students will use learning strategies to extend their communicative competence" (Goals 1 and 3, Standard 3) and "Students will use appropriate learning strategies to construct and apply academic knowledge" (Goal 2, Standard 3). Learning strategies provide English language learners avenues for exploring, processing, testing, and confirming language.

Teachers, by scaffolding instruction and assessment for English language learners, offer students the means to practice and use a variety of strategies in varied contexts (Echevarria, Vogt, & Short, 2000). By knowing their students, teachers can readily select the most appropriate strategies for direct instruction. Ultimately, students, in their use of learning strategies, will gain the confidence to become independent, self-regulated, and self-monitored learners.

For beginners, reading strategies may be imparted orally with accompanying visual support. Students may demonstrate their understanding by following commands, such as, "Point to the picture that shows what the book is about" or "Show me the large print that tells what happens first." More proficient English language learners may share examples of specific strategies, such as predicting what comes next, with their peers.

Instructional and assessment strategies should also include test-taking and study skills. English language learners with limited formal schooling, for example, need to be able to practice strategies as in following teacher directions that are supported by transparencies or other relevant materials and then using the strategies with guidance (as in the common practice of having to transpose information from text to a multiple-choice format). More proficient English language learners should be able to apply strategies, such as explaining how to eliminate incorrect responses or distracters. With test-taking strategies in hand, English language learners are ready to tackle subject matter content without teachers fearing that the format for responding will confound the results.

Interaction With Partners or in Small Groups

Interactive support is helpful to English language learners who benefit from opportunities to practice their new language with a variety of models in different situations. Various ways in which adults, teachers, or students may provide interactive support when speaking with English language learners include the following:

- Repeating or rephrasing the utterance
- Clarifying what is said
- Paraphrasing the message
- Dissecting the message in meaningful chunks
- Offering additional examples or details
- Checking for understanding at frequent intervals
- Combining interactive with visual or graphic supports
- Confirming understanding through use of the native language

In communicating with others, active and sustained involvement of students is generally built into the interaction. When engaging in conversation, personal interest, motivation, social, and affective factors facilitate language acquisition. It is advantageous for English language learners to have interactive support. Through sharing and exchanging learning experiences, languages, and cultures, their language and content bases are broadened.

Cooperative learning structures, described in the previous chapter, offer teachers easy formats for prompting student interaction, whether in pairs or small groups, in native languages or in English. English language learners must become familiar and comfortable with the use of cooperative structures as instructional tools before they are applied to an assessment situation. Depending on the purpose, instructional assessment within the classroom setting may include the whole class, small groups, or individual students. However, accountability for academic achievement or language proficiency should ultimately rest on individual student performance.

CONTINUITY OF SUPPORT FROM THE CLASSROOM TO A LARGE-SCALE LEVEL

As educators, we understand the importance of classroom supports in everyday instruction of English language learners. Any modification of instruction that depends on supports to bolster the students' access to meaning should carry over from the classroom to **large-scale assessment**. The following tips are useful in differentiating instruction and then matching it with assessment:

- Embed meaning in diagrams, photographs, line art, or other forms of visual representation
- Refer to tables, charts, or other forms of graphic representation for information
- Incorporate definitions of difficult words or idiomatic expressions within the same sentence
- Bold key terms or expressions
- Use active tense; avoid passive voice
- Include experiences relevant to students' lives
- Connect cultures and encourage cross-cultural communication
- Reduce excessive (not necessarily redundant) language
- Minimize cultural, linguistic, and class bias
- Permit bilingual dictionaries, glossaries, and use of the native language, as feasible

Some of these modifications, such as the treatment of bias, may be captured through universal **test** design (Thompson, Johnstone, & Thurlow, 2002). Others, as in the use of glossaries or dictionaries, may appear as **accommodations** on large-scale state tests. English language learners with learning disabilities may have other specific accommodations for instruction and assessment written into their individualized education plan, or IEP. These accommodations are to be honored at both the classroom and large-scale levels.

The reflection in Appendix 7.2 is a checklist of best practices for instructing English language learners based on the use of supports. As a teacher, think about how each feature can support classroom or large-scale assessment or both. Then share with a colleague examples of some of these features from your personal experiences.

The concluding section of the chapter discusses student **self-assessment** and reflection as a type of support for English language learners. Students, themselves, as they grow into becoming self-advocates will come to understand their own and best ways of learning. Self-assessment is the means to accomplish that goal.

STUDENT SELF-ASSESSMENT

Student self-assessment has been endorsed by researchers and practitioners alike (Ainsworth & Christinson, 1998; Brown, 2004; O'Malley & Pierce, 1996). English language learners, in particular, should have opportunities to reflect, in their native language or English, on the processes and products of learning. Self-assessment is of value because of how it benefits students:

- It provides a venue for students to convey their depth of understanding.
- It invites students to take responsibility for their own learning.
- It honors student input in the assessment process.
- It recognizes the student perspective as a valid data source.
- It fosters the creation of a shared set of expectations between teachers and students.

- It encourages students to do their best work.
- It helps students set realistic goals based on their accomplishments.
- It offers personalized feedback to teachers.
- It promotes students becoming life time learners.

Student self-assessment is a natural outgrowth of **classroom assessment** where students are the creators of original work. By being student centered, it facilitates self-regulated learning and promotes direct involvement. Student self-assessment, as an extension of performance **activities**, **tasks**, or **projects**, also responds to English language proficiency and/or **academic content standards**.

The concept of student self-assessment may be alien to some English language learners, especially older students who have been schooled outside the United States where student voice is not acknowledged. Teachers should gradually introduce this idea, perhaps initially as a whole-group language experience. Later, individual students can express their thoughts on learning through interactive journal writing where teachers provide feedback, prior to engaging in self-assessment independently.

A Criterion-Referenced Model of Student Self-Assessment

One model for student self-assessment focuses on the standards-based criteria that shape or define the work products and the steps students take to produce evidence of learning. In this model, teachers formulate a series of questions or statements that guide students to produce a response or work sample that conforms to the criteria or specifications of the task. For young students or those with lower levels of language proficiency, responses for self-assessment may be confined to answering yes/no questions or smiling/frowning faces. For older students or those with more developed language proficiency, **rating scales** may be an appropriate form to use for self-assessment.

The examples of student self-assessment in this chapter have been adapted from a formative English language arts portfolio designed for Delaware's English language learners (Gottlieb, 2001). The primary purpose of this classroom-based, instructional assessment tool is to complement the large-scale, secure measure by providing teachers ways of systematically documenting the performance of their English language learners on an ongoing basis.

Table 7.4 is a checklist that mirrors the **language objectives** of a Grade 3 task where beginning English language learners are to identify the elements of story grammar through multicultural storytelling. Following a structured interview with family members of questions that parallel the criteria in the rubric, English language learners are asked to share an oral folk tale from their home culture with classmates. For self-assessment, the students write the name of their folk tale and the country or region from which it came. The teacher or more proficient students read the questions on the checklist and the students circle their responses.

Table 7.4   Storytelling Self-Assessment Checklist

My Folk Tale: _____

Country: _____

1. I know **where** the story takes place (**setting**).	YES	NO
2. I know **when** the story takes place (**time**).	YES	NO
3. I know **who** the people (**characters**) are in the story.	YES	NO
4. I can talk about (**describe**) the people (**characters**).	YES	NO
5. I can tell (**describe**) what happens (**events**) in the story.	YES	NO
6. I can tell (**describe**) what happens in the end (**conclusion**) of the story.	YES	NO

A Reflective Model of Student Self-Assessment

A second model of student self-assessment centers on how students react or feel as a result of participating in a task or project. In this approach, teachers create a set of open-ended questions or statements that prompt higher-order thinking. Students may summarize what they have done (by drawing, speaking, or writing), describe their favorite or most challenging activity, or explain some aspect of learning. In their reflection, depending on the authenticity or real-life application of the task or project, students may assume the role of mathematician, scientist, historian, or researcher. Table 7.5 is an example of student self-assessment at the middle grades built into science class where English language learners reflect on their experiences as inventors at the completion of a project. Students are invited to respond to the questions independently or in small groups, either by writing a narrative or responding orally, in their native language or English, depending on how instruction has been delivered.

Table 7.5   Inventor Self-Assessment Questions

What was the question or hypothesis you wanted to answer?

Did your hypothesis lead to an interesting invention? Why or why not?

Did you like inventing something to test your hypothesis? Why or why not?

How do you feel like an inventor?

Would you like to continue your exploration as an inventor? Why or why not?

Student self-assessment can be incorporated into any content area or **language domain**. The second example of reflective self-assessment is taken from a unit of instruction for high school English language arts. In Table 7.6, English language learners think about the usefulness and application of having compiled a personal résumé as they respond to the questions.

Table 7.6   Résumé Self-Assessment Questions

Was making a résumé important to you? Why or why not?

How does making a résumé prepare you for life after high school?

How do you plan to use your résumé? When might you use it?

What did you discover about yourself in making your résumé?

A Combined Model of Self-Assessment

The two models of self-assessment (product and process) can be combined into one. In it, students respond to whether they completed each activity or specification of the task (as in Model 1) and then reflect on the most gratifying or challenging aspect (as in Model 2). An example of a combined model is from middle school where English language learners follow a step-by-step process to compose a biography. In Table 7.7, Part 1 is a standards-based checklist for students to assist them in completing and then evaluating the task; Part 2 consists of an open-ended question.

Student Self-Assessment as Information Gathering and Feedback

There are times when teachers would have a better sense of what their students are able to do if only they would ask. There is no reason why English language learners cannot be a part of this information-gathering process. The objective is to collect accurate, relevant, even insightful data about students; therefore, teachers of English language learners should consider modifying questions or formats, reading surveys aloud, or allowing students to respond in their native language.

Narrative forms of self-assessment are another venue for gaining the student perspective. Less proficient English language learners may begin to delve into student self-assessment through graphic organizers, such as a KLWH (what I <u>K</u>now, what I <u>L</u>earned, what more I <u>W</u>ish to learn, and <u>H</u>ow I plan to learn it) chart. Teachers gain a sense of students' depth of understanding as well as their use of metacognitive strategies. More proficient English language learners may maintain learning logs in their content classes. These logs, whether teacher directed through leading questions

Table 7.7   Biography Self-Assessment

Biography of _____

Part 1: Here are the steps for creating your biography. Put an X next to ones you did.

☐ I wrote a list of persons who I admire and respect. Then I chose a person to study.
☐ I collected information on the person from two sources (books, the Internet, newspapers, magazines). I included
  • personal information
  • important life events
  • contributions to society
☐ I made a chart of the similarities and differences about the person from the two sources.
☐ I summarized the information from the two sources.
☐ I found pictures about the life of the person.
☐ I used the information to write a 1- to 2-page biography with pictures.

Part 2: Why is the person you chose for the biography important to you? What did this person do to change the way you think or act? Write a paragraph of 3 or 4 sentences.

---

or student self-directed, offer students nonthreatening, yet structured, opportunities to write about their content-related experiences. Teachers respond to students' entries in a manner similar to journal writing to create an ongoing, interactive dialog.

Peer Assessment

All too often, teachers dominate and control speech within a classroom, leaving few opportunities for English language learners to interact among themselves in meaningful discussion. **Peer assessment** is an effective means for having English language learners practice academic language with each other that is grounded in standards and tied to a lesson's or unit's activities. Table 7.8 illustrates one way for teachers to guide peer assessment in the area of language arts for the primary grades.

Peer assessment may be added to that of students and teachers, offering another perspective. Most **rubrics**, checklists, or rating scales can readily be converted (by adding columns) to represent these three data sources. Because they use the identical criteria for assessment, the results provide rich data for student-teacher conferences and feedback for the students. Table 7.9 shows how to collect feedback on assessment from multiple perspectives; in this checklist for oral reports, peers and the teacher have input in the process.

Table 7.8   An Example of Peer-Assessment for Story Writing

Teacher says to the students: "You drew and wrote a story with three parts. Now you are going to share what you did with a partner. Count off in twos. I will start with number 1s and then number 2s."

Number 1s. Tell your partner the name of your story.
Number 2s. Let your partner tell you theirs.

Number 1s. Tell your partner about the beginning of your story.
Number 2s. Let your partner tell you about theirs.

Number 1s. Tell your partner about the middle of your story.
Number 2s. Let your partner tell you about theirs.

Number 1s. Tell your partner about the end of your story.
Number 2s. Let your partner tell you about theirs.

Number 1s. Tell your partner the favorite part of your story.
Number 2s. Let your partner tell you about their favorite part.

Table 7.9   An Oral Report: Feedback From Students and the Teacher

Who are you? A student listener_____   The teacher listener_____

Who is speaking? _____

What is the title of the oral report? _____

What is the date? _____

Listen to the speaker. Then read the sentences. Put an X on YES or NO.

1. The speaker began the report with the title.	YES	NO
2. I understood what the speaker said.	YES	NO
3. The speaker used pictures or objects to help explain what was said.	YES	NO
4. The speaker used body language to help explain what was said.	YES	NO
5. The speaker introduced the topic at the beginning of the report.	YES	NO
6. The speaker gave details or examples.	YES	NO
7. The speaker gave a summary at the end.	YES	NO
8. I think I could retell what the speaker said.	YES	NO

LARGE-SCALE STUDENT SELF-ASSESSMENT

Student self-assessment or reporting, for the most part, is not incorporated in large-scale assessment. However, the test that has served as the nation's report card since 1969, the National Assessment of Educational Progress (NAEP) has systematically collected student-level background data. Information on students' literacy and math practices in background questionnaires is analyzed to provide context to the national report (NAEP, 2003a, 2003b).

Presented in a multiple-choice format, the reading and writing survey for fourth-grade NAEP asks questions about reading and writing pastimes, the types of literacy materials used by students outside of school, and the frequency of literacy assignments within school. In addition, it asks how often a language other than English is used in the home (National Center for Education Statistics [NCES], 2003).

On the math questionnaire for eighth-grade NAEP, questions range from the use of calculators to the math classes students expect to take in high school. In addition, there is a series of math-related statements. Students report the extent to which they agree, on a five-point scale, that math is useful, involves complex problem solving, and is enjoyable and whether they consider themselves good in the subject area (NCES, 2003).

SUMMARY AND FINAL THOUGHTS

English language learners, by definition, need sustained support to enhance their access to and make meaning of the language and content they encounter in school. Teachers use different kinds of support, presented in visual, graphic, or interactive forms, to scaffold and differentiate instruction and assessment. In addition, English language learners, through student self-assessment, have viable, enabling tools that allow them to be vested in the learning process.

All students can increase their understanding of language and content from visually supported text, graphic organizers, and self-assessment. Proficient English students use various supports to confirm text-based information or, as an intermediary step, on their way to produce a work sample. English language learners, on the other hand, rely more heavily on graphics and visuals as their primary source for processing and demonstrating their understanding and, perhaps, even as the end products of their work. It is the responsibility of educators to build the bridges between curriculum, instruction, and assessment to enable every student to thrive in school.

APPENDIX 7.1

Features of Graphic Organizers for English Language Learners

Does the graphic organizer . . .	YES	NO
1. Reflect English language proficiency standards and/or academic content standards for the grade level?		
2. Focus on a curricular kernel or big idea?		
3. Exemplify the unit's or lesson's content or language objectives?		
4. Promote higher levels of cognitive engagement while reducing the language load?		
5. Offer ways of making information more accessible, meaningful, and connected?		
6. Serve as a means of arranging information as a preview for presenting it in more extended discourse (either orally or in writing)?		
7. Describe what students can do, given their levels of English language proficiency?		
8. Represent what students can do, given their age, experiential backgrounds, and exposure to modeling and use of the organizer?		
9. Facilitate the acquisition of language and learning of content?		
10. Provide a means of increasing the motivation of students to accomplish a task?		

APPENDIX 7.2

REFLECTION: Features of Classroom and Large-Scale Assessment

Think about how you approach assessment in your classroom for your English language learners. Share some examples of these features with a colleague. Then decide whether these same approaches apply to large-scale assessment in your school district or state. Again, compare your responses with those of your colleague.

Feature	Classroom Assessment	Large-Scale Assessment
1. The linguistic complexity of oral or written discourse is adjusted.		
2. Language is supported with graphic representation.		
3. Language is supported with visual representation.		
4. Language proficiency measures social and academic language.		
5. Academic achievement measures the knowledge and skills of the subject matter.		
6. Students have time to interact with each other.		
7. Language is supported with authentic materials and manipulatives.		
8. The activity or task is geared to students' level of English language proficiency.		
9. The activity or task is anchored in English language proficiency and/or academic content standards.		
10. Students engage in higher-level thinking to accomplish a task.		
11. The students' use of learning strategies is taken into account.		
12. Students have opportunities to self-assess and reflect on their learning.		

8

Standardized Testing and Reporting

The Bridge to Fair and Valid Assessment

Politicians promise to build bridges even when there are no rivers.

—Nikita Khrushchev

Standardized testing is the most common form of **summative assessment** that contributes to educational accountability. The issue of the use of **standardized tests** is fraught with controversy for English language learners. This chapter seeks to portray a balance among the various avenues of **assessment** and, in doing so, explores viable approaches that schools may use for reporting information on English language learners' **language proficiency** and **academic achievement**.

STANDARDIZED TESTING

There has been ongoing debate over the appropriateness of standardized testing for any student. Sacks (1999) argues that standardized tests are an artifact of the eugenics movement (an attempt to sort people based on their perceived intelligence through testing), whose spirit remains institutionalized in the American belief system. Shohamy (2001) addresses the misuses of language tests—in particular, their negative effects—and the consequences for stakeholders; she ultimately calls for limiting the power of **tests** and protecting the rights of test takers. Kamii (1990) contends that although the use of standardized tests is problematic altogether, the most deleterious effects are on preschool and primary grade students.

These arguments have been supported by a host of organizations and agencies. The National Center for Fair and Open Testing has been a persistent opponent to standardized testing, claiming that **performance assessment** is a more equitable and authentic means of accountability for both teachers and students. Others specifically oppose the use of high-stakes tests and their sanctions. The U.S. Department of Education's Office for Civil Rights (2000) has been critical of the misuse of high-stakes testing from an equity standpoint, whereas the American Educational Research Association (2000) has admonished high-stakes testing on the basis of evidence gathered from scientifically based research.

Numerous teacher organizations have joined the cry for testing reform and have issued policy statements or resolutions to this effect (International Reading Association, 1999; National Council of Teachers of English, 2000; National Council of Teachers of Mathematics, 2000a; National Education Association, 2004-2005; Teachers of English to Speakers of Other Languages, 2000, 2003) Many have taken the stance that overdependence on the results from single test for educational decision making is irresponsible. The use of **multiple measures** is the only rational recourse for counteracting this practice.

Yet standardized testing remains a time-honored tradition of schooling. National legislation, such as the Elementary and Secondary Education Act, of which No Child Left Behind is the latest enactment, has elevated the status and significance of the testing in American schools. As such, we, as educators, must rationalize how best to deal with these mandates that have been externally imposed from a federal, state, or school district level.

Standardized tests are designed to measure a broad band of competencies, whether for academic achievement, such as language arts, mathematics, or science, or, in the case of English language learners, for English language proficiency as well. Standardized tests are outside the direct control of teachers and removed from **classroom assessment**. However, all teachers need to be knowledgeable about standardized testing and understand how the data affect teaching and learning. The pros and cons for using standardized tests are outlined in Table 8.1.

Norm-Referenced and Criterion-Referenced Tests

There are generally two types of standardized, large-scale tests. **Norm-referenced tests** rank students by measuring their relative performance against that of the norm

Table 8.1   The Advantages and Disadvantages of Using Standardized Tests

Advantages	Disadvantages
• Produce reliable data	• Often serve as a gatekeeper
• Insist on uniform data collection and analyses	• Represent shallow curricula, not broad, in-depth knowledge
• Provide a national perspective or ranking	• Don't allow for student creativity or imagination
• Are not confounded by individual teacher effects	• Don't take different student learning styles into account
• Often are readily scored	• Adhere to time limits
• Easy to train teachers on procedures for administration	• Lead to misinterpretation of data and overgeneralization of results

group. **Criterion-referenced tests,** on the other hand, gather information about student progress or achievement in relation to a specified criterion. In a standards-based assessment model, the standards serve as the criteria or yardstick for measurement.

The primary advantage of criterion-referenced measures is that they allow us to make inferences about how much language proficiency, in the case of language proficiency tests, or knowledge and skills, in the case of academic achievement tests, that students initially have (their baseline) and their subsequent gains over time. Criterion-referenced tests are concerned with the extent to which students have mastered the performances (represented in the standards) along a continuum rather than ranking students on a bell curve. Thus, for English language learners, with a criterion-referenced model, we are able to see their individual growth from year to year.

Use of Data From Standardized Tests

Some standardized tests provide both criterion-referenced and norm-referenced information. It is important that teachers, students, parents, administrators, and boards of education understand the purpose of the tests and how the results are to be used. Scores on tests often contribute to decisions regarding student eligibility for services, **reclassification**, grade-level promotion, or even graduation. When there are consequences for students, teachers, or schools stemming from these actions, standardized tests become high-stakes in nature.

Teachers need to be knowledgeable of the different ways standardized test results are reported, how to interpret the numbers or scores, and how best to communicate what they mean. Norm-referenced standardized tests can produce the following types of results:

- **Raw scores** (total number of correct items)
- **Stanines** (equal-interval scores where the bell curve is evenly divided into nine segments)

- **Percentiles**, deciles, or quartiles (nonequal interval data determined from a mean and standard deviation of a normal distribution of scores)
- Normal curve equivalents (equal interval data where the bell curve is evenly divided into ninety-nine segments)
- Standard or z scores (number of standard deviations the score is from the mean)
- **Grade-level equivalents** (identification of student development using grade level as a marker).

Figure 8.1   Types of Standardized Scores and Their Distribution Along the Bell Curve

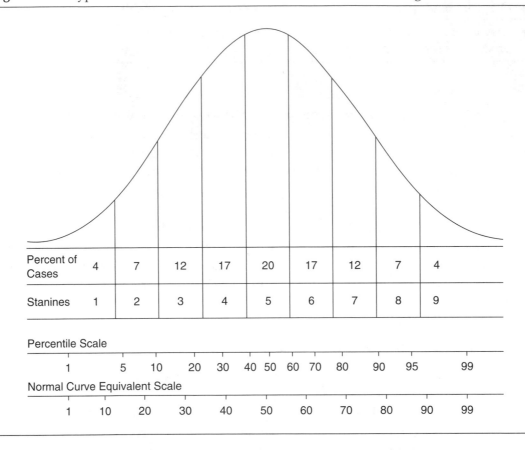

Percent of Cases	4	7	12	17	20	17	12	7	4
Stanines	1	2	3	4	5	6	7	8	9

Percentile Scale

1   5   10   20   30   40 50 60 70   80   90   95   99

Normal Curve Equivalent Scale

1   10   20   30   40   50   60   70   80   90   99

Large-scale, standardized norm-referenced tests are built around "normal distribution" on a bell curve. As shown in Figure 8.1, numerous types of scores are derived from slicing the bell-shape curve into intervals or segments. Each one shows how individual students fare in relation to the norm group.

With the availability of so many different types of scores for norm-referenced standardized tests, which ones are most appropriate and useful? What do they tell us about our students? Appendix 8.1 offers advantages and disadvantages of using the most common score types.

The results of standardized achievement tests appear to be less suitable for low-achieving students, with **English language learners** being a prime example of such a group. Their scores may be contaminated by lack of interest or motivation coupled with frustration (Fradd & McGee, 1994). In addition, students' self-worth and feelings of self-efficacy are negatively affected; so much so, that the benefits of information gained from testing may be negated (Paris, Lawton, Turner, & Roth, 1991).

These issues are compounded for English language learners for whom standardized academic achievement tests have not been conceptualized or developed. Because most measures are literacy dependent and available only in English, we simply don't know the extent to which students' English language proficiency influences their achievement. Even with a strong conceptual base in their **native language** or additional **supports** in English, until English language learners reach a threshold of English language proficiency, they will be unable to demonstrate their true achievement in their second language.

REFLECTION: Information on Standardized Tests

Scout out a technical manual for a test of academic achievement. In it, there should be information on how the test was developed, the norming population, and what types of scores are used to interpret the results. Look for the following information about the test.

- What is its purpose?
- When was it developed?
- On how many students was it normed? How many were English language learners? What were their levels of English language proficiency?
- Which language/cultural groups were included?
- Were bias and content reviews conducted that examined how items might impact English language learners?
- Which types of scores are used? What do they mean?
- Are there any specific **accommodations** for English language learners? Have they been researched?
- Share your findings with other teachers. Decide if the test is appropriate for English language learners and if it will yield useful information.

STANDARDIZED TESTING AND ENGLISH LANGUAGE LEARNERS

English language learners are subject to standardized tests as are all other students; unfortunately, the results are often not true indicators of their performance. If the tests themselves are not valid for our students, neither are the inferences made from them. Consequently, their worth, especially under high-stakes conditions, comes into question.

Standardized Testing of Academic Achievement

Historically, tests of academic achievement have not served our students well. However, the standards-based movement and federal legislation have given English language learners national recognition and have included our students in school and statewide accountability. Teachers who work with English language learners now have leverage in insisting on rigorous, standards-based curriculum that can be differentiated by language proficiency levels. We must also ensure that large-scale, standardized tests for our students, based on that curriculum, are fair, valid, and useful.

The lack of **validity** of standardized tests of academic achievement for English language learners, especially with lower levels of English language proficiency, stems from various sources. The reasons extend across the test development process, from conceptualization of the blueprint to test construction to administration to data analysis and reporting. The following list of statements reflects the primary faults of standardized tests of academic achievement for English language learners that lead us to question their validity.

- Universal design does not guide test development.
- The developmental nature of the **second language acquisition** process is not taken into account in item construction.
- Language complexity and density confound students' ability to express conceptual understanding.
- Access to meaning or understanding is dependent on print.
- Bias and content review panels have not focused on linguistic or cultural influences on the items.
- Pilot and field-testing do not include ample representation of English language learners across various language proficiency levels.
- Modifications or accommodations for English language learners and those with disabilities are not piloted, field-tested, or empirically examined.
- English language learners being schooled in their native language do not have comparable, parallel standards-based native language tests to demonstrate their achievement.

On the basis of the information in a technical report on a measure of academic achievement (as in the reflection), it should be apparent that our English language learners are generally not well represented in standardized tests of academic achievement. If per chance they are, the distribution of different languages and cultures represented may not coincide with the student populations in your school or school district. Therefore, we must be cautious in interpreting the results.

Reporting Results of Standards-Based Tests of Academic Achievement

Reporting results on the academic achievement of English language learners must be contextualized to be meaningful. That is, academic performance, especially if measured in English, should be presented in relation to the student's level of English language proficiency. For that reason, Tables 8.2 and 8.3 have parallel formats; teachers need to understand the relationship between a student's English language proficiency and academic achievement and the influence of the former on the latter.

Table 8.2 is a format for a hypothetical report that assumes students are tested in four content areas of four standards each. The state, in this case, has a **designation** system where results are posted for five performance levels. **Standard scores** are inserted into a student's performance level. Working from the premise that some English language learners are relatively new to the country, sections of the report have been whitened out to indicate that an accommodated or alternate version of the test has been administered.

Accommodations for English Language Learners on Standardized Tests of Academic Achievement

Sometimes tests of academic achievement have suggested accommodations, or modifications to the test or setting that do not affect validity, for English language learners. Teachers who may be administering these tests should make sure that the accommodations reflect the instructional modifications offered English language learners in general education classrooms and have been researched on this student population. The most common accommodations for English language learners used by states in large-scale assessment include the following:

- Extended testing time
- Small-group administration
- Individual administration
- Oral reading of questions in English (except the reading test)
- Use of bilingual lists and dictionaries (Rivera, Stansfield, Scialdone, & Sharkey, 2000)

REFLECTION: Matching Instructional Modifications to Accommodations

Make a list of ways in which you and other teachers modify instruction for English language learners. Now, find a copy of your state policy regarding the kinds of accommodations allowable in administering tests of academic achievement. Does your list match the state's policy? How might you make adjustments to your instruction based on the policy?

The purpose of accommodations is to enhance student participation in and performance on **large-scale assessment**s (Butler & Stevens, 1997). However, there is an underlying assumption that all English language learners are advantaged from their

Table 8.2 A Hypothetical Standards-Based Report for Academic Achievement

	State Performance Levels (as in California) based on Academic Content Standards																			
Content Areas	*Level 1 (Far Below Basic)* Academic Content Standard				*Level II (Below Basic)* Academic Content Standard				*Level III (Basic)* Academic Content Standard				*Level IV (Proficient)* Academic Content Standard				*Level V (Advanced)* Academic Content Standard			
Language arts	1*	2	3	4	1	2	3	4	1	2	3	4	1	2	3	4	1	2	3	4
Mathematics	1	2	3	4	1	2	3	4	1	2	3	4	1	2	3	4	1	2	3	4
Science	1	2	3	4	1	2	3	4	1	2	3	4	1	2	3	4	1	2	3	4
Social studies	1	2	3	4	1	2	3	4	1	2	3	4	1	2	3	4	1	2	3	4

* Each academic content standard and definition of the performance levels are to be stated on the back, in English and the student's native language.

implementation and that the students would benefit from assessment in general education classrooms under similar conditions. If you give me a test in Russian, for example, it doesn't matter how much time you give me, whether the questions are read to me, or if I take the test with a small group of peers, I will not profit from the accommodations. Research is needed to develop guidelines for determining when versions of assessments, other than "standard" English, should be administered (August & Hakuta, 1997).

Alternate Assessment of Academic Achievement

English language learners with severe cognitive disabilities may qualify to take an **alternate assessment** of academic achievement, if stipulated in their individualized education plan (IEP). This assessment reflects a different set of standards that have been designed specifically for students with special needs. Each state should have alternate assessment in place for this subset of students. It is important to consider the unique characteristics of English language learners for those students who have both language and learning needs.

Alternate assessment, although generally used for students with special needs, may also refer to different approaches to assessing English language learners' academic achievement. Most common is administering a test in the student's native language. However, several states are investigating alternate forms of assessments in English for which even an accommodated assessment would not yield accurate information. Some innovative, alternate ways of assessing achievement may include the following:

- Use of different **selected response** types, other than multiple choice
- Reduction of linguistic complexity, but retention of redundancy
- Rich graphic and visual support
- Technology driven or computer adaptive testing
- Presentation of English and native language in the same instrument

Standardized Language Proficiency Testing

The No Child Left Behind Act of 2001 insists that states' English language proficiency tests, given annually to K through 12 English language learners, be grounded in English **language proficiency standards**. To meet federal requirements, this new generation of standardized language proficiency tests needs to change radically from the previous one. What has happened is that currently retooled or newly developed English language proficiency tests have come to share many of the traits of those of academic achievement. Appendix 8.2 compares the features of the two generations of language proficiency tests.

Reporting Results of English Language Proficiency Tests

Just as there are distinctions between language proficiency and academic achievement, there are differences between these two types of standardized tests. Language proficiency tests are intended to mark students' annual progress in English language development as they move toward the ultimate goal of attainment of English language proficiency standards. Tests of academic achievement measure students' knowledge and skills in relation to meeting grade-level content standards.

Table 8.3 illustrates one way to report English language proficiency results that parallels the one for academic achievement (in Table 8.2). In this generic model, there are four English language proficiency standards and five levels of English language proficiency presented across the four **language domain**s (borrowed from the WIDA [World-Class Instructional Design and Assessment] Consortium). The identical format can display student, class, grade-level cluster, district, or statewide data. Individual cells can mark student data from the state test, yielding a profile of language competencies for each standard.

Standardized Testing and Accountability for English Language Learners

Accountability rests with schools and states that have substantial numbers of English language learners. For this ever-increasing student population, there are three dimensions to federal accountability, two that address English language proficiency and one for academic achievement.

1. Annual progress in English language proficiency

2. Attainment of English language proficiency

3. Meeting state academic content standards

The sole source of these determinations, in most states, is their standardized test data on English language proficiency and academic achievement.

Bilingual and **English as a second language** educators agree on the universal goal that all students reach high standards and applaud the recognition of English language learners as part of statewide accountability. Nevertheless, issues distinct for English language learners require special scrutiny and consideration. Abedi and Dietel (2004) succinctly present a list of these concerns, based on their research:

• Testing performance of English language learners
• Accuracy in measurement
• Instability of the group
• Additional variables that impact performance outside of schooling

First, it's a fact that English language learners' performance is not commensurate with their English-proficient peers; that's a primary characteristic in identifying these students. Second, the validity of standardized tools for English language learners has come under serious question. Next, English language learners are not like other subgroups with identifiable, unalterable characteristics such as gender, race/ ethnicity, or even severe cognitive disabilities; their designation changes on attaining and maintaining English language proficiency. In addition, English language learners tend to be mobile, with some of these students being migrant. Last, research has

Table 8.3 A Hypothetical Standards-based Report for English Language Proficiency (ELP)

	English Language Proficiency Levels (as in the WIDA Consortium)																			
	Level I (Entering)				Level II (Beginning)				Level III (Developing)				Level IV (Expanding)				Level V (Bridging)			
Language Domains	ELP Standard				ELP Standard				ELP Standard				ELP Standard				ELP Standard			
Listening	1*	2	3	4	1	2	3	4	1	2	3	4	1	2	3	4	1	2	3	4
Speaking	1	2	3	4	1	2	3	4	1	2	3	4	1	2	3	4	1	2	3	4
Reading	1	2	3	4	1	2	3	4	1	2	3	4	1	2	3	4	1	2	3	4
Writing	1	2	3	4	1	2	3	4	1	2	3	4	1	2	3	4	1	2	3	4

*Each academic content standard and definition of the performance levels are to be stated on the back, in English and the student's native language.

repeatedly shown that there are conditions, outside of school, that generally have a negative influence on school performance—namely, lower levels of family income and parent education.

Given these issues that surround the accountability of English language learners, how best can we comply with federal and state regulations while offering fair and equitable assessments? Among the recommendations suggested by Abedi and Dietel (2004), as by others (cited throughout the book), is the use of multiple measures.

Use of Multiple Measures

Multiple measures represent varying perspectives as to what is valued in teaching and learning. Complementing large-scale and classroom measures invites teachers to become vested in the process and have input into accountability of their students. The reliance on information on more than one measure affords English language learners various opportunities to demonstrate their true competencies.

Multiple Measures of Academic Achievement

Accountability systems can be configured in numerous ways. Because English language proficiency is the most recognizable and distinguishing variable for English language learners, it should serve as a mediator for both assessment and grading. Table 8.4 exemplifies how to adjust the demands of accountability for English language learners' academic achievement according to their levels of English language proficiency.

In this fictional example, three types of measures contribute to accountability: standardized achievement tests, standard performance **tasks**, and a standard classroom protocol. Standardized tests match students' academic profiles and take into account their native or English language development. Likewise, standard performance tasks, created at a state level, vary in accordance with students' English language proficiency. The state-specific, standards-based classroom protocol allows teachers to have input as well.

The weight of the measures (expressed as a range in percentages) reflects students' English language proficiency levels. Accountability for students at the beginning stages of English language proficiency should be less dependent on standardized tests, whereas that for those English language learners ready to transition from support services should mirror the expectations of their proficient English peers. Standard performance tasks, geared to English language learners, allow students to engage in more authentic, long-range **activities** and **projects**. The classroom protocol provides summary information derived from the students' overall performance, perhaps demonstrated through a portfolio or compendium of original work samples.

Multiple Measures of English Language Proficiency

An annual, state English language proficiency test is a staple in the arsenal of assessment measures for English language learners. However, the usefulness of

Table 8.4 Suggested Measures for Academic Achievement for English Language Learners (ELLs) in Grades 3 Through 12 and Their Range of Contribution to Accountability

For English Language Proficiency Levels 1–2			
Types of measures	Standardized tests of academic achievement in the native language (if instruction is in L1) or alternate measures in English designed and normed on ELLs	Standard set of performance tasks in L1 (if instruction is in L1) or L2	Classroom protocol based on performance in L1 or L2
Range	10–40%	10–50%	10–40%

For English Language Proficiency Levels 3–4			
Types of measures	Standardized tests of academic achievement in English designed and normed on ELLs or state standardized tests of academic achievement with validated accommodations	Standard set of performance tasks in L1 or L2	Classroom protocol based on performance in L1 or L2
Range	30–60%	10–40%	10–30%

For English Language Proficiency Level 5			
Types of measures	State standardized tests of academic achievement with validated accommodations	Standard set of performance tasks in L2	Classroom protocol based on performance in L2
Range	40–60%	10–40%	0–20%

Table 8.5 Suggested Measures of Accountability for English Language Proficiency by Grade-Level Cluster With Ranges Assigned to Oral Language and Literacy Development

Grade-Level Cluster	Measures: Standardized test of English language proficiency, standard set of language proficiency tasks in English, and classroom observation of students' performance in English	
	Range Assigned to Oral Language (Listening and Speaking)	*Range Assigned to Literacy (Reading and Writing)*
K–1	70–80%	20–30%
2–3	50–60%	40–50%
5–8	30–40%	60–70%
9–12	10–20%	80–90%

subjecting young students to standardized testing, especially in the areas of reading and writing, has come under fire. Therefore, other developmentally appropriate tools, such as observation **checklists** or assessment portfolios, can supplement testing results.

Table 8.5 offers suggested weights for oral language and literacy measures for English language proficiency by grade-level cluster. The types of measures for English language proficiency parallel those for academic achievement; that is, standardized testing is complemented with standard tasks and a classroom tool. For students in enrichment or dual-language programs, the table may also serve as a guide for assessing proficiency in two languages.

The ranges of percentages in the table reflect the relative importance that oral language and literacy play in general education classrooms. For younger students and students with limited formal schooling, emphasis is initially on oral language development while literacy in English is being established. For older students, literacy plays a more vital role while oral language is introduced and reinforced.

When multiple measures are introduced into an accountability system, sustained professional development for teachers must follow. Teachers must have standard procedures for collecting and analyzing classroom-based data, including uniform **rubrics** for interpreting student work. In addition, sets of student anchor papers from performance tasks are helpful in guiding the process.

SUMMARY AND FINAL THOUGHTS

For English language learners and their teachers, accountability is more comprehensive than for **proficient English students** because it encompasses both language proficiency and academic achievement. Assessment of English language learners, especially in this era of accountability, is complex, and results need to be framed in a context that considers students' native language, culture, and English language proficiency. Therefore, teachers must have familiarity with how standardized tests are constructed and how student data are reported.

We want to ensure that the evidence used for accountability is an expression of standards, curriculum, and instruction and, most important, representative of student learning. Multiple measures for both language proficiency and academic achievement provide English language learners diverse ways to demonstrate their language and academic competencies. The bridge to fair and equitable assessment for our students can be constructed only if we create an all inclusive educational system.

APPENDIX 8.1

The Pluses and Minuses of Using Different Types of Scores From Norm-Referenced Standardized Achievement Tests

Type of Scores	Pluses	Minuses
Raw scores	Most easy to compute	Carry no meaningful information (e.g., a score of 55 . . . out of how many?); no comparability across forms
Grade-level equivalent scores	Seductive as expressed in grade levels; however, recommended to be eliminated due to misunderstanding (Airasian, 1991)	Most readily misinterpreted (e.g., a fourth-grader's reading score is at grade-level 8.2 . . . but it does not mean the student can read eighth-grade material)
Normal curve equivalents	Most readily understood	Not used to a wide extent
Percentiles	Most realistic interpretation; relate the percentage of the norm group the student surpassed	Assumption that there are equal intervals between percentiles when there aren't
Stanines	Most holistic estimate	Not as precise as percentiles or normal curve equivalents
Standard scores or z scores	Most historically associated with norm-referenced testing	Population specific

APPENDIX 8.2

Comparison of Features of Standardized English Language Proficiency Tests Pre/Post the No Child Left Behind Act of 2001

	Pre NCLB	*Post NCLB*
Primary purpose	Screening, classification, and redesignation	Accountability
Theoretical base	Tied to acquisition of social language	Tied to acquisition of social and academic language within schooling
Criteria for measurement	Performance of proficient English peers in relation to the language acquisition process	Performance of students in relation to English language proficiency standards
Use of data	Initial identification, placement, and monitoring progress	Meeting progress expectations and attainment of English language proficiency standards
Stakes	Low; nonsecure tests	High; secure tests

9

Grading Systems

The Bridge to the Future

I am where I am because of the bridges that I crossed.

—Oprah Winfrey

Grading goes hand in hand with schooling; it is a form of individual student accountability. Although the standards movement has shifted our focus, and perhaps the criteria we use, grading is inevitably a mainstay of American education. With increasing numbers of students who are English language learners, teachers need to carefully reexamine how they make judgments about student performance.

This chapter highlights how grading and reporting systems can be designed to reflect the accomplishments of English language learners. In it, we explore ways to represent standards-based teaching and learning. Finally, we suggest the use of student portfolios as a means of accumulating documentation over time of our students' language development and **academic achievement**.

THE ISSUE OF GRADING

While **assessment** is based on interpretation of data, grading is more evaluative. Other factors outside academic performance are often considered, such as effort, motivation, timeliness, and presentation of work. English language learners, by definition, cannot compete academically with their proficient English peers in English, so how can grades realistically convey what they have learned?

Grading Students of the Same Level of English Language Proficiency

Sometimes **English language learners** are grouped into classes, especially at the high school level, according to their level of English language proficiency. The following scenario and reflection are about assigning grades to two English language learners in their high school **English as a second language** (ESL) class (adapted from A. Katz, personal communication, August 2004). As teachers, we should think about the factors that influence our grading practices and what we would want to communicate to these students about their learning.

Ana is in an intermediate ESL class. She attends regularly and always comes on time. However, she participates in class activities only reluctantly and completes very few homework assignments. She rarely contributes to group work or class discussions. Yet she manages to do fairly well on classroom **tests**, the midterm, and the final exam.

Carlos is in the same intermediate class. Several times during the term, he arrives after class has started because he often works late. He tackles each homework assignment and tries his best to complete the work. He makes an effort to engage in class activities and consistently contributes to group work. However, his downfall is the final exam. He can't seem to relate what he knows, especially on an important test.

REFLECTION, PART 1: The Dilemma of Grading

At the end of the semester, Ana and Carlos receive the grades displayed in Table 9.1. In this instance, letter grades are used, but they could just as easily be number grades. Based on this scenario, what final grade would you give these students for the semester and why? (A = highest grade; F = lowest grade)

Actually, it is difficult to determine the semester grade for these students because we do not know the criteria that constitute each component. Teachers should relate to students from the beginning what each component means and how much (in terms of percentage or points) each one contributes to the overall grade. As Guskey and Bailey (2001) point out, the primary goal of grading and reporting is communication and, in this instance, that is not clear.

REFLECTION, PART 2: Clarifying the Meaning of Grades

So let's examine Table 9.1 again. This time you may want to answer the following questions to communicate clearly to the students what their grade means.

- Which standards are being assessed?
- Are students being assessed on their listening, speaking, reading, and/or writing?
- What is the weight of each component (e.g., are quizzes and tests 40%, classroom assessments 40%, and the other two components 10% each)?
- What is expected for classroom performance and homework assignments?

Whatever is decided, the information has to be shared with students at the beginning of the grading period so that there is a common understanding of grading procedures.

Table 9.1   Hypothetical Semester Grades in ESL for Two Intermediate-Level High School English Language Learners

	Ana	Carlos
Quizzes, midterm, and final exam	B	D
Classroom-based assessments (including contributions to group work)	C	B
Classroom performance (including behavior and attitude)	D	B
Homework assignments	D	B

Grading English Language Learners With Varying English Language Proficiency Levels

In the previous scenario, the two students happened to be at approximately at the same level of English language proficiency. But how do teachers grade newly arrived English language learners who are in the same grade level and classroom as ones who are ready to transition into general education classes? Teachers at the elementary and middle school levels often work with groups of heterogeneous English language learners.

We differentiate instruction and assessment according to English language learners' proficiencies in English (and their **native language**); this premise has to extend to grading as well. Thus, the primary purpose for grading students at the lower end of the English language proficiency continuum should be to document their progress in English language development. Students and teachers have to set realistic language and content goals in English (and the native language, whenever applicable) within a marking period. For example, students with limited formal schooling cannot be expected to move at the same pace as those English language learners with a solid educational foundation. In turn, it would be an injustice to subject our students to the identical criteria as those who have been raised exclusively in an English-speaking environment.

The main purpose for grading English language learners at the higher end of the **language proficiency** scale is to ascertain the extent to which these students are meeting standards and approaching parity with their English proficient peers. Thus, achievement is stressed over progress. At this time, it is justifiable to use uniform criteria for grading these two groups of students.

Using multiple data sources for grading is appropriate for all students, including English language learners. However, the relative weight of each form of assessment (or data source) may be adjusted by language proficiency level, teacher discretion, and district policy. Within a grading system, there should be representation of the following:

- Student **self-assessment** (the older the students, the greater responsibility they should take for their own learning)
- Performance assessment (where students have opportunities to demonstrate learning through **task**s and **projects** that are interpreted by **rubrics**)
- More traditional testing procedures (all student need to gain familiarity with different testing formats)

Table 9.2 proposes different weights (expressed in percentages) for each data source according to students' grade-level cluster. This information should be used in conjunction with that in Table 8.4, where suggested percentages are attached to measures by English language learners' levels of English language proficiency. Ultimately, for second-language learners, **classroom** and **large-scale assessment** ought to serve complementary functions.

Table 9.2 A Suggested Contribution (in percentages) of Data Sources for Purposes of Grading English Language Learners at Different Grade-Level Clusters

Types of Measures	Student Self-Assessment	Performance Assessment With Rubrics	Paper-and-Pencil Tests
Grade levels K–2	5%	85%	10%
Grade levels 3–5	10%	75%	15%
Grade levels 6–8	15%	60%	25%
Grade levels 9–12	20%	50%	30%

Grading as a Reflection of Standards-Based Teaching and Learning

Guskey and Bailey (2001) recommend tying grades to statements of purpose that, in turn, are matched with evidence. If our purpose and evidence are standards driven, can traditional grading practices be kept? Probably not. With school districts and teachers painstakingly restructuring assessment, curriculum, and instruction, grading, too, must become standards referenced.

Suppose students in Grades 3 through 5 were working on an integrated theme, "Getting Products to Market." For English language proficiency, the teacher selects an assortment of reading and writing **strands** from various English **language proficiency standards**. From those, she writes **language objectives** and then repeats the process for academic achievement, drawing from the state's **academic content standards** to create **content objectives**.

Tables 9.3 and 9.4 show an example of how to reorganize grading English language learners according to their language proficiency level using English language proficiency standards as a backdrop for an instructional assessment project. In Table 9.3, we see the standards and performance indicators that are addressed for grading. In Table 9.4, we assign a range of points (or percentages) that apply to each language proficiency level.

The higher the language proficiency level, the greater the contribution of standards-based learning to the total score and grade; conversely, there is less dependence on non-standards-based factors. Using this example as a template, teachers can insert state English language proficiency standards, **language domains**, and performance indicators addressed in teaching for **summative assessment**; the total score can then be converted to a grade for their English language learners at their designated language proficiency level.

Grading must provide clear feedback to students and their parents. At the same time, it must support standards-based learning. As such, grading, by providing useful information that centers on what English language learners can do, becomes a communication system that facilitates informed decisions and actions (Trumbull & Farr, 2000).

The Report Card: Grading English Language Proficiency and Academic Achievement of English Language Learners

English language learners are acquiring language and learning content simultaneously; therefore, both language proficiency and academic achievement have to be represented in reporting their grades. Language proficiency must be graded in English (and another language, if students are participating in a dual-language program). Content area instruction that serves as the basis for academic achievement, on the other hand, may proceed in English, the students' native language, or a combination of both. This information must be clearly specified in a report card.

English language proficiency and academic achievement should be presented side by side on a report card; Table 9.5 shows one way of displaying grades for English language learners. If instruction is being provided in the students' native language, the content areas that apply need to be designated (note the two columns on the academic achievement side for languages). In that way, teachers, students, and parents are able to see how students are performing in relation to their given level of English language proficiency.

Table 9.3 English Language Proficiency Standards Addressed in a Classroom Project Designed for English Language Learners of Various Language Proficiency Levels in Grade-Level Cluster 3 Through 5

English Language Proficiency Standards	Language Proficiency Level 1	Language Proficiency Level 2	Language Proficiency Level 3	Language Proficiency Level 4
Language of English language arts: reading	Match labels or identify facts from pictures	Identify language associated with stating facts from illustrated text	Identify language associated with stating opinions from illustrated text	Differentiate between statements of fact and opinion
Language of English language arts: writing	List personal information	Describe personal information or experiences	Compare/contrast personal experiences	Compose personal narratives
Language of mathematics: reading	Match words or pictures with math symbols	Match illustrated words or phrases with math-related terms	Select examples of language of math-related terms and information from illustrated text	Summarize language of math-related terms and information
Language of social studies: reading	Match illustrations and labels of goods and services to geographic locations	Identify features of goods and services depicted in illustrated phrases or short sentences	Compare/contrast goods and services using graphic organizers	Interpret effects of goods and services on people's lives

Table 9.4 A Proposed System for Grading English Language Learners Using a Range of Points at Various English Language Proficiency Levels

English Language Proficiency Level	Language Proficiency Level 1	Language Proficiency Level 2	Language Proficiency Level 3	Language Proficiency Level 4
Points from performance assessment of standards	0–20	21–40	41–60	61–80
Self-assessment points	0–10	0–10	0–10	0–10
Teamwork and personal responsibility points	0–35	0–25	0–15	0–5
Motivation and effort points	0–35	0–25	0–15	0–5
Grand total of possible points	100	100	100	100

USING STUDENT PORTFOLIOS FOR ASSESSMENT AND GRADING

Student portfolios are representations of their accomplishments in school. There are many different kinds of portfolios (showcase portfolios of best work, pivotal portfolios of most important work, and collections of work samples, to name a few), and each one has a distinct purpose. We limit our discussion here to the assessment portfolio, a systematic collection of the processes and products of original student work and their associated documentation (Gottlieb, 1995) and how it helps contribute to grading English language learners.

If assessment portfolios are part of a grading scheme at a classroom or large-scale level (school, district, or state), then certain procedures are necessary to ensure their care, maintenance, and **reliability**. If all teachers at a given grade level are using the identical criteria in grading and evaluating student work, then the potential uses of the portfolio are expanded. A student's assessment portfolio that has been assigned grades based on English language proficiency and academic content standards can be helpful for teachers who have English language learners who may be the following categories:

- Transferring schools within a district
- Reclassified into a new English language proficiency level
- Eligible for transitioning from support services
- Considered for prereferral to special education (Pierce & O'Malley, 1992)

Table 9.5   A Sample Standards-Based Report Card for English Language Learners

English Language Proficiency

Student's English Language Proficiency Level: _____

	Social language	Language of math	Language of science	Language of social studies	L2
Listening					
Speaking					
Reading					
Writing					

Academic Achievement

	L1	L2
Language arts		
Math		
Science		
Social studies		

Throughout this book, we have emphasized the importance of **classroom assessment** and how it contributes to our understanding of English language learners. Assessment portfolios are a venue by which this information can be stored and maintained over time. In this way, we will have documentation and evidence (in addition to standardized measures) of the progress of our students.

Features of Assessment Portfolios

Since the 1990s, educators have advocated the use of assessment portfolios for English language learners (Farr & Trumbell, 1997; Gómez, 1998; Navarrete, 1990; Richard-Amato & Snow, 2005). Portfolios should be designed to simultaneously capture English language learners' language proficiency and academic achievement through **performance assessment**. Thus, by centering on authentic contexts for teaching and learning, assessment portfolios can represent the following:

- Learning in students' native language and/or English
- Interdependence between oral language and literacy development
- Integration of language and content
- Higher-level thinking through extended tasks and projects
- Students' personal reflections and self-assessment

Assessment portfolios should be portraits of the students—who they are, what they can do, and how they communicate their knowledge. For grading purposes (especially on a large-scale level, such as within a district), there might be restrictions in terms of the types and numbers of entries required or how student work is interpreted. However, if assessment portfolios are to be valued, students need to have a voice and ownership in their contents.

Contents of Assessment Portfolios

There is tremendous variability in the contents of portfolios and how the samples of student work are selected for assessment and grading purposes. Figure 9.1 is a continuum that illustrates a range of possibilities as to who has input and how assessment portfolios are configured. Teacher philosophies, instructional practices, and district policy all come into play in the decision process.

Figure 9.1   A Continuum of Voices in an Assessment Portfolio

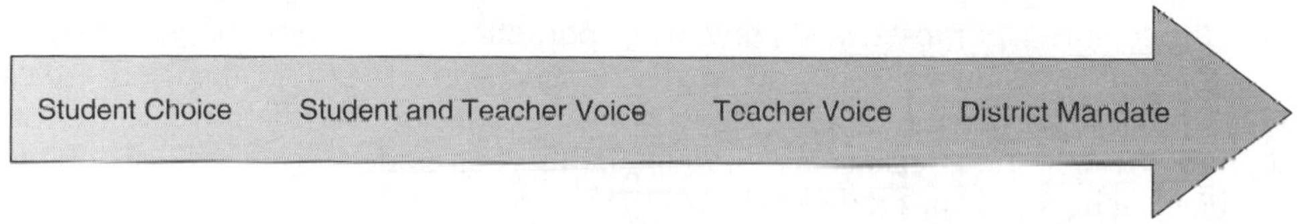

Student Choice   Student and Teacher Voice   Teacher Voice   District Mandate

Students may have choice, within a set of general guidelines, as to what goes into their portfolios. In this type of assessment portfolio, students may use their portfolios to collect all their original work during a grading period and then select their best or most representative pieces to be graded. When students and teachers each have input, both may contribute to reach a joint decision as to the portfolio's contents. In the third case, teachers may be very systematic and uniform in the selection of standards, work samples, and rubrics to be used for grading. Last, a school district may impose how an assessment portfolio is organized, which work samples and rubrics are included, and when entries are to be collected and perhaps require the inclusion of standardized measures.

In designing assessment portfolios for English language learners, teachers need to consider students' ages, levels of English language proficiency, and familiarity with handling portfolios. For students with lower levels of English language proficiency or for those who have had limited formal schooling, a more structured portfolio is necessary. Once students gain familiarity with the routine of using portfolios as a reservoir of their learning, they can gradually have more freedom in their choices.

General Types of Entries

Assessment portfolios should mirror standards, curriculum, and the languages of instruction in proportion to their use. It is important that the portfolios are thoughtfully organized so that there is continuity from marking period to marking period or articulation from year to year. Assessment portfolios that are used for grading English language learners might contain the following entries:

1. A student summary sheet (see Tables 9.2 and 9.3) with
   - teacher and student goals
   - English language proficiency and academic content standards
   - evidence of student work (in narrative or list form)

2. Original samples of student work with accompanying rubrics or narrative feedback

3. Multimedia entries

4. Quizzes and tests

5. Peer and student self-assessment or reflection on the collective body of work

---

REFLECTION: Portfolio Use

Review the features, purposes, and contents of portfolios. Which type of portfolio might be best for your teaching style and your English language learners? Take the list of the contents and provide concrete examples of how you and your students might create an assessment portfolio. Use the **checklist** in Appendix 9.1 as your guide. Discuss your conclusion with other teachers at your grade level.

Multimedia Entries

With assessment portfolios, English language learners have opportunities to present evidence of learning in varied formats, according to their interests, learning style, or English language proficiency level. The increased availability of technology affords teachers and students more choices. There is a sampling of ideas for incorporating multimedia into portfolios in the following box.

Ideas for Multimedia Entries in an Assessment Portfolio

- Digital writing samples and reflections (stored on a CD or disk)
- Scanned pieces of creative work
- PowerPoint presentations
- Photographs of models or exhibits
- Collages or other artistic renderings
- Videotapes of reenactments, dramatizations, or student interaction
- Audiotapes of oral language samples or oral reading
- Evidence of use of computer programs or computer-based research

---

Reporting Grades Through Portfolio Conferences

Assessment portfolios are the perfect venue for students to showcase their newly acquired language and knowledge as well as to share their accomplishments with others. One-on-one conferences can be arranged at the close of a marking period to organize the contents, review the entries, and set common goals for the coming months. In that way, the grades that are ultimately assigned have personal meaning to the students and their family members.

Guidelines as to how to set up the portfolio should be embedded in instruction (O'Malley & Pierce, 1996). Teachers should have a management plan for portfolios where decisions regarding the quantity (how many entries), quality (which rubrics or documentation forms), timing (when entries are to be submitted), and presentation (in chronological order, by content area, or by language) are decided. Depending on their age, students may create a table of contents and design the cover to reflect their personal interests.

Teacher-Student Conferences

Students' involvement in the creation of their portfolios carries over to conferencing with their teachers. For English language learners with mid to high levels of English language proficiency or in bilingual settings where their native language is used, student-led conferences are feasible. For English language learners with lower levels of English language proficiency, the teacher should guide the students. In either instance, some key questions form the basis of the conference. The following suggestions may be considered by teachers for a conference with their students.

Teacher-Student Conferences

- Show me your best work. Tell me why you chose this piece. What did you learn from doing it? Let's look at your goals this marking period. What grade do you think you should get. Why? Show me the evidence that this is the grade you deserve.
- Show me your portfolio. Tell me what you did in each piece. Which one are you most proud of? Why? What grade do you think you should get for math (or any content area)? What was your goal and did you reach it this marking period? What goal should we work on next?
- Let's look at your goals this marking period. How has your English improved? Show me a piece from the beginning of the year and one you just finished. Tell me how you are a better reader (listener, speaker, writer). What grade do you think you should get? Why?

The conference should strengthen individualized instruction and the bond between teacher and student (Farr & Tone, 1994). Afterward, teachers may complete the summary sheet (Tables 9.6 and 9.7) for their English language learners to supplement (or supplant) the school's report card. Grades are entered for English language proficiency and academic achievement in reference to the given standards. In addition, there is space to write a short narrative based on the evidence and a description of the student's attitude and effort.

Table 9.6   Side 1 of a Hypothetical Summary Sheet for an Assessment Portfolio Used for Grading English Language Learners

Student: _____ Grade Level: _____

Quarter: _____ Year: _____ Teacher(s): _____

English language proficiency level: _____

English language proficiency standards		Grade in L2 (English)		Goals and evidence:
	Listening			
	Speaking			Effort and attitude:
	Reading			
	Writing			
Academic content standards	Language arts	Grade in L1	Grade in L2	Goals and evidence:
	Math			
	Science			Effort and attitude:
	Social studies			

Table 9.7   Side 2 of a Summary Sheet: Sample Criteria for a Standards-Referenced Portfolio

Based on the evidence in the portfolio, mark 1, 2, or 3 to indicate whether the student is addressing, approaching, or attaining the indicated set of standards.

	1-3	1—Addresses Standards	2—Approaches Standards	3—Attains Standards
English language proficiency		• Work remains at same level of quality over time	• Work quality shows clear progress and growth over time	• Work quality exemplifies that expressed in grade-level standards
Academic achievement in L1 (if applicable)		• Little or weak evidence • Skills/concepts/ideas sporadically or loosely linked	• Inconsistent evidence • Skills/concepts/ideas communicated meaningfully	• Strong, supported evidence • Skills/concepts/ideas integrated and applied to new situations
Academic achievement in L2		• Few reasoning or learning strategies	• Variety of reasoning or learning strategies	• Full repertoire of reasoning or learning strategies for grade level

Family Member Conferences

Family members of English language learners cannot readily communicate in English and are probably not familiar with the American school system. "Portfolio Nights," where students come to school with family members to share their portfolios, are a welcome way of encouraging school involvement. Students take the lead in preparing their portfolios and developing key questions in English and their native language, with their teacher's assistance, to use when displaying their portfolios (e.g., *¿Quieres ver mi mejor trabajo?* Do you want to see my best work?). In this way, English language learners take pride and ownership in their portfolio while their parents or other family members gain insights into what children do at school.

A follow-up teacher/family member/student conference then becomes a powerful tool. In it, teachers may show typical portfolios of students (whose names are removed) along with documentation forms. Family members and students alike will be able to inspect actual work samples, compare them with the student's, reach their own conclusions, and then propose goals for the rest of the year. There is a more complete understanding of the expectations of teaching and learning when grades are attached to specified criteria and work samples.

SUMMARY AND FINAL THOUGHTS

Historically, grading students has been a rather subjective exercise. It has been most challenging for teachers to assign grades to English language learners whose English language proficiency may preclude them from accessing content and demonstrating their true knowledge. In recent years, standards have provided teachers guidance in identifying teaching and learning objectives, deciding how to measure them, and translating the results into grades. For English language learners, English language proficiency and academic content standards offer the criteria for grading students' language proficiency in English and academic achievement in English or native language.

Assessment portfolios are one way in which students and teachers can gather information and provide evidence for learning. This collection of student work, including standard rubrics and student self-assessment, is the documentation of English language learners' progress over time. It also serves as a communication tool for students, family members, and teachers.

Our English language learners cross many bridges in their educational careers. For assessment, we must ensure that our students have clear and well-marked pathways to success. As educators, it is our responsibility to prepare our English language learners to reach their potential and brightest future.

APPENDIX 9.1

An Assessment Portfolio Checklist

This checklist may be helpful in planning the design and contents of your assessment portfolio to use in grading your English language learners.

Considerations

- ☐ The students' ages
- ☐ The students' levels of English language proficiency
- ☐ The students' prior experiences with portfolios
- ☐ The language(s) of instruction for

Language arts	L1	L2
Mathematics	L1	L2
Science	L1	L2
Social studies	L1	L2

- ☐ Student input, including attitude and effort
- ☐ English language proficiency and academic content standards addressed

Contents

- ☐ A student summary sheet
- ☐ Teacher and student goals and standards
- ☐ Original samples of student work with accompanying rubrics or narrative feedback
  - o English language proficiency—oral language
  - o English language proficiency—literacy
  - o Academic achievement—language arts
  - o Academic achievement—mathematics
  - o Academic achievement—science
  - o Academic achievement—social studies

- ☐ Multimedia, including cassette tapes, computer disks, photographs
- ☐ Peer and student self-assessment or reflection

Glossary

Academic achievement: demonstration of learning that is directly tied to the knowledge and skills embedded in the curriculum of specific content areas

Academic content standards: descriptions of the goals of student achievement for designated curriculum areas

Academic language proficiency: the language patterns and concepts required in understanding, processing, and communicating curriculum-based content

Accommodations: modifications to a test or setting that do not affect the validity of the measure, intended to assist English language learners or students with disabilities

Activity: an instructional assessment component that consists of a series of related questions or a single in-depth question that generally corresponds to a language or content objective and is relatively short in duration

Alignment: the match or degree of correspondence between two entities, such as between sets of standards or between assessment and instruction

Alternate assessment: applicable to students with disabilities or those English language learners with lower levels of English language proficiency, these approaches are intended to measure standards on a large-scale basis in ways other than regular state tests

Analytic scale: a type of developmental rubric, usually in the form of a matrix, in which a construct is defined by its dimensions or traits and the levels of performance

Assessment: the systematic, iterative process of planning, collecting, analyzing, reporting, and using student data from a variety of sources over time

Bilingual education: support services for English language learners in which the students are instructed in their native language for some portion of the day in order to learn grade level concepts and achieve academically

Checklist: a dichotomous scale (with two options) or rubric where traits, language functions, skills, strategies, or behaviors are marked as being either present or absent

Classroom assessment: the planning, collection, analysis, and reporting of information that is an outgrowth of instruction and unique to teachers

Constructed response: types of assessment or test items where the students supply the answers or produce original work

Content objective: the component of a lesson design that addresses the knowledge and skills of a curricular area to be addressed in instruction and assessment

Content stem: the element of a performance indicator that relates its topic or context

Content-based instruction: a set of strategies and teaching techniques for English language learners that integrates language with concepts that are associated with specific content areas

Criterion-referenced test: a type of measure that is based on established criteria, such as standards, rather than ranking the performance of students

Designation: the classification scheme used to define a student's level of language proficiency or academic achievement

Discrete point measures: tests that are skill-based or where skills are presented in isolation

Dual language education: a form of enrichment education where English language learners learn side-by-side with proficient English students and instruction is delivered in two languages

English as a second language: a generic term that may apply to a program, content area, curriculum, or instruction targeted for English language learners

English language learners (or English learners or English speakers of other languages): linguistically and culturally diverse students whose English language proficiency precludes them from accessing, processing, or learning grade-level material in English

Evaluation: using the evidence from assessment data to judge the worth or effectiveness of students or services

Formative assessment: the ongoing collection, analysis, and reporting of data used to provide immediate feedback to students and inform instruction

General education program: services provided to students who are proficient English speakers without additional support

Grade-level equivalent: a type of test score that defines student performance using grade level as the marker

Holistic scale: a type of developmental rubric in which there is an overall description of competencies for each performance level

Home language survey: a form or series of questions, usually incorporated into school registration, that identifies whether students come from a linguistically and culturally diverse background where they are exposed to another language and culture in daily interaction

L1: a student's first or native language

L2: a student's second language, usually English

Language domain: the arbitrary division of language into the areas of listening, speaking, reading, or writing

Language function: the way in which language is used to communicate a message

Language objective: the component of a lesson design that addresses the language domains and language functions to be incorporated into instruction and assessment

Language proficiency: a person's competence or ability to process and use language across the language domains

Language proficiency standards: descriptions of the goals for students in marking progress along the second language acquisition continuum to attaining full proficiency

Large-scale assessment: the use of standard or uniform conditions across multiple classrooms (departments, grade levels, schools, districts, or states) in the planning, collecting, analyzing, and reporting of student data

Level of language proficiency: a defined stage in the developmental progression that constitutes the second language acquisition process

Manipulatives: the use of objects as part of instruction to introduce and reinforce concepts

Multiple measures: the reliance on two or more types of data sources at different points in time to make educational decisions

Native language: the primary language of the home; generally, the first language a student acquires

Normal curve equivalents: a statistic descriptive of results from a standardized, norm-referenced test in which the bell curve has been divided into ninety-nine equal segments or intervals

Norm-referenced measure: a type of test where student scores are ranked by performance and distributed along a bell curve

Peer assessment: feedback on student work from other students from the same grade level or class

Percentile: a test statistic determined from a mean and standard deviation of a normal distribution of scores that represents non-equal interval data

Performance assessment: the collection of original student work generated from real-life situations, such as in tasks and projects, that is embedded in instruction and usually interpreted with rubrics

Performance or progress indicators: sample observable and assessable descriptions of what students can do to demonstrate progress toward or attainment of a standard

Proficient English students: linguistically and culturally diverse students who are former English language learners or those students for whom English is their home or native language

Project: a comprehensive representation of instructional assessment that consists of a series of related or scaffolded tasks and allows students to explore a topic in depth

Rating scale: a type of rubric where traits, language functions, skills, strategies, or behaviors are defined by their frequency of occurrence (how often) or quality (how well)

Raw score: the total number of correct items on a test

Reclassification: the change of status in a student's designation; at the time of transitioning from support services, English language learners are reclassified as proficient English students

Reliability: the internal cohesiveness of a measure, the uniformity of interpretation from rater to rater, or the consistency of the results

Rubrics: scoring guides or documentation forms with specified criteria used to interpret student work

Second language acquisition: a series of predictable, developmental stages that English language learners pass through on their way to gaining full proficiency

Selected response: types of assessment or test items where the possible answers are listed, such as in multiple-choice or true/false.

Self-assessment: opportunities for students to monitor and analyze their work as a means of reflecting on their strategies, products, and processes of learning

Social language proficiency: the language patterns and concepts required in understanding, processing, and communicating thoughts and ideas in daily interaction

Standard portfolio: a uniform collection of student work, used for assessment purposes, that is interpreted and reported with the identical rubrics or criteria

Standard score: a test statistic that denotes the number of standard deviations a score is from the mean or average

Standardized test: a measure designed to be administered, scored, and interpreted in the identical manner, irrespective of when it is given

Stanine: a statistic descriptive of results from a standardized, norm-referenced test in which the bell curve has been divided into nine equal segments or intervals

Strand: a series of performance indicators that scaffold across the levels of language proficiency to show the developmental progression in language acquisition

Summative assessment: the collection, analysis, and reporting of data at designated time frames (such as the end of a semester) used to provide a summary of student performance and to measure program effectiveness

Supports: linguistic, visual, or graphic aids that facilitate language acquisition and academic achievement

Task: an instructional assessment component that consists of a series of related or scaffolded activities that generally corresponds to multiple language or content objectives

Task-specific scales: types of holistic or analytic rubrics that are designed for a single instructional assessment task or project

Test: a systematic procedure for collecting a sample of student behavior or performance at one point in time

Validity: the extent to which the assessment measures and data are appropriate for the decisions to be made about the students; the extent to which a test matches its stated purpose

References

Abedi, J., & Dietel, R. (2004, Winter). Challenges in the No Child Left Behind Act for English Language Learners. *CRESST Policy Brief, 7.* Retrieved July 22, 2005, from www.cse.ucla .edu/products/newsletters/policybrief7.pdf

Ainsworth, L., & Christinson, J. (1998). *Student-generated rubrics: An assessment model to help all students succeed.* Orangeburg, NY: Dale Seymour.

Airasian, P. W. (1991). *Classroom assessment.* New York: McGraw-Hill.

American Educational Research Association. (2000, July). *AERA position statement concerning high-stakes testing in pre-K-12 education.* Washington, DC: Author.

Arter, J., & McTighe, J. (2001). *Scoring rubrics in the classroom: Using performance criteria for assessing and improving student performance.* Thousand Oaks, CA: Corwin.

August, D., Calderon, M., & Gottlieb, M. (2004, October). *How to design science-based instructional systems for achieving academic English and content.* Paper presented at Office of English Language Acquisition's "Celebrate Our Rising Stars" Summit III, Washington, DC.

August, D., & Hakuta, K. (Eds.). (1997). *Improving schooling for language-minority children: A research agenda.* Washington, DC: National Academy Press.

Bachman, L. (1990). *Fundamental considerations in language testing.* Oxford, UK: Oxford University Press.

Bailey, A. L., & Butler, F. A. (2002). *An evidentiary framework for operationalizing academic language for broad application to K-12 education: A design document.* Los Angeles: University of California, Los Angeles, National Center for the Study of Evaluation/National Center for Research on Evaluation, Standards, and Student Testing.

Baker, D. (1989). *Language testing: A critical survey and practical guide.* London: Edward Arnold.

Bauman, J. F., Kame'enui, E. J., & Ash, G. E. (2002). Research on vocabulary instruction: Voltaire redux. In J. Flood, D. Lapp, D. R. Squire, & J. Jensen (Eds.), *Handbook of research on the teaching of English language arts* (pp. 752–785). Mahwah, NJ: Erlbaum.

Brisk, M. E., & Harrington, M. M. (2000). *Literacy and bilingualism: A handbook for ALL teachers.* Mahwah, NJ: Lawrence Erlbaum.

Brown, H. D. (2004). *Language assessment: Principles and classroom practices.* White Plains, NY: Pearson.

Buck, G. (2001). *Assessing listening.* Cambridge, UK: Cambridge University Press.

Butler, F. H., & Stevens, R. A. (1997). *Accommodation strategies for English language learners on large-scale assessments: Student characteristics and other considerations* (CSE Technical Report 448). Los Angeles: University of California, Los Angeles, National Center for the Study of Evaluation/National Center for Research on Evaluation, Standards, and Student Testing.

Carrasquillo, A. L., & Rodriguez, V. (2002). *Language minority students in the mainstream classroom* (2nd ed.). Tonawanda, NY: Multilingual Matters.

Chamot, A. U., & O'Malley, J. M. (1994). *The CALLA handbook: Implementing the cognitive academic language learning approach.* New York: Addison-Wesley.

Christian, D., & Genesee, F. (Eds.). (2001). *Bilingual education.* Alexandria, VA: TESOL.

Cohen, A. D. (1994). *Assessing language ability in the classroom.* Boston, MA: Heinle & Heinle.

Commission on Reading. (1985). *Becoming a nation of readers.* Champaign: University of Illinois, Center for the Study of Reading.

Crandall, J. (Ed.). (1987). *ESL through content-area instruction.* Englewood Cliffs, NJ: Prentice Hall Regents.

Cummins, J. (1981). The role of primary language development in promoting educational success for language minority students. In California State Department of Education (Ed.), *Schooling and language minority students: A theoretical framework* (pp. 3–49). Los Angeles: California State University, Evaluation, Dissemination and Assessment Center.

Cummins, J. (2005, April). *Challenging monolingual instructional assumptions in second language immersion and bilingual programs.* Paper presented at the American Education Research Association annual meeting, Montreal, Canada.

Darian, S. (2003). *Understanding the language of science.* Austin: University of Texas Press.

Darling-Hammond, L., Ancess, J., & Falk, B. (1995). *Authentic assessment in action.* New York: Columbia University, Teachers College Press.

Dixon, C. N., & Nessel, D. (1983). *Language experience approach to reading (and writing).* Hayward, CA: Alemany Press.

Echevarria, J., Vogt, M. E., & Short, D. J. (2000). *Making content comprehensible for English language learners: The SIOP model.* Boston: Allyn & Bacon.

El Nassar, H. (2003, June 19). 39 million make Hispanics largest U.S. minority group. *USA Today.* Retrieved July 20, 2005, from www.usatoday.com/news/nation/census/2003-06-18-Census_x.htm

Enright, D. S., & McCloskey, M. L. (1988). *Integrating English: Developing English language and literacy in the multilingual classroom.* Reading, MA: Addison-Wesley.

Eskey, D. E., & Grabe, W. (1988). Interactive models for second language reading: Perspectives on instruction. In P. Carrell, J. Devine, & D. Eskey (Eds.), *Interactive approaches to second language reading.* Cambridge, UK: Cambridge University Press.

Estrada, P. (2004). Patterns of language arts instructional activity and excellence in first- and fourth-grade culturally and linguistically diverse classrooms. In H. C.Waxman, R. G. Tharp, & R. S. Hilberg (Eds.), *Observational research in U.S. classrooms* (pp. 122–143). Cambridge, UK: Cambridge University Press.

Ewy, C. A. (2002). *Teaching with visual frameworks: Focused learning and achievement through instructional graphics co-created by students and teachers.* Thousand Oaks, CA: Corwin.

Farr, B. P., & Trumbull, E. (1997). *Alternate assessments for diverse classrooms.* Norwood, MA: Christopher-Gordon.

Farr, R., & Tone, B. (1994). *Portfolio and performance assessment: Helping students evaluate their progress as readers and writers.* Fort Worth, TX: Harcourt Brace.

Finocchiaro, M., & Brumfit, C. (1983). *The functional-notational approach: From theory to practice.* New York: Oxford University Press.

Fradd, S. H., & McGee, P. L. (1994). *Instructional assessment: An integrated approach to evaluating student performance.* Reading, MA: Addison-Wesley.

Freeman, Y. S., & Freeman, D. (2000). *Teaching reading in multicultural classrooms.* Portsmouth, NH: Heinemann.

Genesee, F. (1987). *Learning through two languages: Studies of immersion and bilingual education.* Cambridge, MA: Newbury House.

Genesee, F., & Upshur, J. A. (1996). *Classroom-based evaluation in second language education.* Cambridge, UK: Cambridge University Press.

Glatthorn, A. A. (1998). *Performance assessment and standards-based curricula: The achievement cycle.* Larchmont, NY: Eye on Education.

Gómez, E. L. (1998). *Perspectives on policy and practice: Creating large-scale assessment portfolios that include English language learners.* Providence, RI: Education Alliance at Brown University.

Gómez, E. L. (2000). A history of the ESL standards for pre-K–12 students. In M. A. Snow (Ed.), *Implementing the ESL standards for pre-K-12 students through teacher education* (pp. 49–74). Alexandria, VA: Teachers of English to Speakers of Other Languages.

Gottlieb, M. (1995). Nurturing student learning through portfolios. *TESOL Journal, 5*(1), 12–14.

Gottlieb, M. (1999a). *The language proficiency handbook: A practitioner's guide to instructional assessment.* Springfield: Illinois State Board of Education.

Gottlieb, M. (1999b). Assessing ESOL adolescents: Balancing accessibility to learn with accountability for learning. In C. J. Faltis & P. Wolfe (Eds.), *So much to say: Teenagers, bilingualism and ESL at the secondary school* (pp. 176–201). New York: Teachers College Press.

Gottlieb, M. (2000). *Standards-based alternate assessment for limited English proficient students: A guide for Wisconsin educators* [CD ROM]. Madison: Wisconsin Department of Public Instruction.

Gottlieb, M. (2001). *Delaware's Portfolio Assessment for Limited English proficient Students: Language arts formative assessment tasks.* Dover: Delaware State Department of Education.

Gottlieb, M. (2002). *Wisconsin alternate assessment for students with limited English proficiency: Teacher's guide.* Madison: Wisconsin Department of Public Instruction. Retrieved from www.dpi.state.wi.us/dpi/dlsea/equity/biling.html

Gottlieb, M. (2003). Large-scale assessment of English language learners: Addressing accountability in K-12 settings. *TESOL Professional Papers #6.* Alexandria, VA: Teachers of English to Speakers of Other Languages.

Gottlieb, M. (2004a). How do we assess English language learners? In *On our way to English: Teacher's Guide.* Barrington, IL: Rigby.

Gottlieb, M. (2004b). *WIDA consortium English language proficiency standards for English language learners in kindergarten through grade 12: Overview document.* Madison: State of Wisconsin.

Gottlieb, M., & Hamayan, E. (2002). Assessing oral and written language proficiency: A guide for psychologists and teachers. In R. B. Vega (Ed.), *Serving English language learners with disabilities* (www.isbe.net). Springfield: Illinois State Board of Education.

Gottlieb, M., & Hamayan, E. (in press). Assessing language proficiency of English language learners in special education contexts. In G. B. Esquivel, E. C. Lopez, & S. Nahari (Eds.), *Handbook of multicultural school psychology.* New York: Lawrence Erlbaum.

Gottlieb, M., & Nguyen, D. (2004). Developmental bilingual education in the real world: Using longitudinal data to enhance dual language program development. *Proceedings from the 4th International Symposium on Bilingualism,* Tempe, AZ.

Guskey, T. R. (Ed.). (1994). *High stakes performance assessment: Perspectives on Kentucky's educational reform.* Thousand Oaks, CA: Corwin.

Guskey, T. R., & Bailey, J. M. (2001). *Developing grading and reporting systems for student learning.* Thousand Oaks, CA: Corwin.

Halliday, M. A. K. (1976). *System and function in language.* London: Oxford University Press.

Hein, G. E., & Price, S. (1994). *Active assessment for active science.* Portsmouth, NH: Heinemann.

Hill, B. C. (2001). *Developmental continuums: A framework for literacy instruction and assessment K-8.* Norwood, MA: Christopher-Gordon.

Hyerle, D. (1996). *Visual tools for constructing knowledge.* Alexandria, VA: Association for Supervision and Curriculum Development.

Hymes, D. H. (1972). On communicative competence. In J. B. Pride & J. Holmes (Eds.), *Sociolinguistics.* Harmondsworth, UK: Penguin.

International Reading Association and National Association for the Education of Young Children. (1998). *Overview of learning to read and write: Developmentally appropriate practices for young children.* Retrieved July 25, 2005, from www.naeyc.org/about/positions/PSREAD0.asp

International Reading Association. (1999). *High-stakes assessments in reading: A position of the IRA.* Newark, DE: Author.

International Reading Association. (2001). *Second-language literacy instruction: A position statement of the International Reading Association.* Retrieved July 25, 2005, from www.reading.org/downloads/positions/ps1046_second_language.pdf

Kagan, S. (1989). *Cooperative learning: Resources for teachers.* San Juan Capistrano, CA: Resources for Teachers.

Kamii, C. (Ed.). (1990). *Achievement testing in the early grades: The games grown-ups play.* Washington, DC: National Association for the Education of Young Children.

Kessler, C., & Quinn, M. E. (1987). ESL and science learning. In J. Crandall, (Ed.), *ESL through content-area instruction.* Englewood Cliffs, NJ: Prentice Hall Regents.

Kindler, A. L. (2002). *Survey of states' limited English proficient students and available educational programs and services, 2000–2001 summary report.* Washington, DC: National Clearinghouse for English Language Acquisition and Language Instruction Educational Programs. Retrieved July 30, 2005, from www.ncela.gwu.edu/policy/states/reports/seareports/0001/sea0001.pdf

Kiplinger, V. L., Haug, C. A., & Abedi, J. (2000, June). *A math assessment should test math, not reading: One state's approach to the problem.* Paper presented at the 30th Annual National Conference on Large-Scale Assessment, Snowbird, UT.

Krashen, S. D. (1992). *The input hypothesis: Issues and implications.* New York: Longman.

Krashen, S. D., & Terrell, T. D. (1983). *The natural approach.* Hayward, CA: Alemany Press.

Kuhn, T. S. (1962). *The structure of scientific revolutions.* Chicago: University of Chicago Press.

Madsen, H. S. (1983). *Techniques in testing.* New York: Oxford University Press.

Manning, M. ., Manning, G., & Long, R. (1994). *Theme immersion: Inquiry-based curriculum in elementary and middle schools.* Portsmouth, NH: Heinemann.

Mohan, B. (1986). *Language and content.* Reading, MA: Addison-Wesley.

Murphy, S., & Underwood, T. (2000). *Portfolio practices: Lessons from schools, districts, and states.* Norwood, MA: Christopher-Gordon.

Nation, I. S. P. (2001). *Learning vocabulary in another language.* Cambridge, UK: Cambridge University Press.

National Assessment of Educational Progress. (2003a). *Mathematics: Student background questionnaire, grade 8.* Washington, DC: National Center for Education Statistics.

National Assessment of Educational Progress. (2003b). *Reading: Student background questionnaire, grade 4.* Washington, DC: National Center for Education Statistics.

National Center for Education Statistics. (2004). *The nations's report card: Background questionnaires.* Retrieved October 15, 2005, from http://nces.gov/nationsreportcard/bgquest.asp

National Clearinghouse for English Language Acquisition and Language Instruction Educational Programs. (2002). *ELL demographics by state.* Retrieved from July 30, 2005, from www.ncela.gwu.edu/stats/3_bystate.htm

National Council of Teachers of English. (2000). *English teachers pass resolution on high-stakes testing and the rights of test takers.* Urbana, IL: NCTE, Public Affairs Office.

National Council of Teachers of Mathematics. (1989). *Curriculum and evaluation standards for school mathematics.* Reston, VA: Author.

National Council of Teachers of Mathematics. (2000a). *High-stakes testing.* Retrieved July 22, 2005, from www.nctm.org/about/position_statements/highstakes.htm

National Council of Teachers of Mathematics. (2000b). *Principles and standards for school mathematics.* Reston, VA: Author.

National Education Association. (2004-2005). *Accountability and testing.* Retrieved September 6, 2005, from www.nea.org/accountability/index.html

National Reading Panel. (2000). *Teaching children to read: An evidence-based assessment of scientific research literature on reading and its implications for reading instruction.* Washington, DC: National Institute of Child Health and Human Development.

National Research Council. (1996). *National science education standards.* Washington, DC: National Academy Press.

Navarrete, C. J. (1990). Reaching out: Using portfolios to combine formal and informal assessments. *EAC-WEST News, 4*(1), 1.

Navarrete, C., & Gustke, C. (1996). *A guide to performance assessment for linguistically diverse students.* Albuquerque: New Mexico Highlands University, EAC West.

Neill, M., Guisbond, L., & Schaeffer, B. (2004). *Failing our children: How "No Child Left Behind" undermines quality and equity in education: An accountability model that supports school improvement.* Cambridge, MA: FairTest.

O'Malley, J. M., & Chamot, A.U. (1990). *Learning strategies in second language acquisition.* New York: Cambridge University Press.

O'Malley, J. M., & Pierce, L. V. (1996). *Authentic assessment for English language learners: Practical approaches for teachers.* New York: Addison-Wesley.

On our way to English: Teacher's guide. (2004). Barrington, IL: Rigby.

Pardo, E. B., & Tinajero, J. V. (1993). Literacy instruction through Spanish: Linguistic, cultural, and pedagogical considerations. In J. Tinajero & A. F. Ada (Eds.), *The power of two languages: Literacy and biliteracy for Spanish-speaking students* (pp. 26–36). New York: Macmillan/McGraw-Hill.

Paris, S. G., Lawton, T. A., Turner, J. C., & Roth, J. L. (1991). A developmental perspective on standardized achievement testing. *Educational Researcher, 20*(5), 12–20.

Peregoy, S., & Boyle, O. (1993). *Reading, writing, and learning in ESL: A resource book for teachers.* White Plains, NY: Longman.

Pierce, L. V. (2001). Assessment of reading comprehension strategies for intermediate bilingual students. In S. J. Hurley & J. V. Tinajero (Eds.), *Literacy assessment of second language learners* (pp. 64–83). Boston: Allyn & Bacon.

Pierce, L. V., & O'Malley, J. M. (1992). *Performance and portfolio assessment for language minority students.* Washington, DC: National Clearinghouse for Bilingual Education.

Rhodes, L. K., & Shanklin, N. L. (1993). *Windows into literacy: Assessing learners K-8.* Portsmouth, NH: Heinemann.

Richard-Amato, P. A. (2003). *Making it happen: From interactive to participatory language teaching* (3rd ed.). White Plains, NY: Pearson Education.

Richard-Amato, P. A., & Snow, M. A. (Eds.). (2005). *Academic success for English language learners: Strategies for K-12 mainstream teachers.* White Plains, NY: Pearson Education.

Rivera, C., Stansfield, C. W., Scialdone, L., & Sharkey, M. (2000). *An analysis of state policies for the inclusion and accommodation of English language learners in state assessment programs during 1998–1999.* Arlington, VA: George Washington University Center for Equity and Excellence in Education.

Sacks, P. (1999). *Standardized minds: The high price of America's testing culture and what we can do to change it.* New York: Perseus Books.

Shearer, A. P., & Homan, S. P. (1994). *Linking reading assessment to instruction: An application worktext for elementary classroom teachers.* New York: St. Martin's.

Shohamy, E. (2001).*The power of tests: A critical perspective on the uses of language tests.* London: Pearson Education.

Short, D. (1993). Assessing integrated language and content instruction. *TESOL Quarterly, 27,* 627–656.

Short, D. J., Gomez, E. L., Cloud, N., Katz, A., Gottlieb, M., & Malone, M. (2000). *Training others to use the ESL standards: A professional development manual.* Alexandria, VA: Teachers of English to Speakers of Other Languages.

Slavin, R. E., & Cheung, A. (2003). *Effective reading programs for English language learners: A best-evidence synthesis* (Report No. 66). Baltimore: John Hopkins University, CRESPAR.

Slavin, R. E., & Cheung, A. (2004). How do English language learners learn to read? *Educational Leadership, 61*(6), 52–57.

Smith, J. K., Smith, L. F., & De Lisi, R. (2001). *Natural classroom assessment: Designing seamless instruction & assessment.* Thousand Oaks, CA: Corwin.

Smith, M. (1986). A model for teaching native oriented science. In J. J. Gallagher & G. Dawson (Eds.), *Science education and cultural environments in the Americas.* Washington, DC: National Science Teachers Association.

Snow, M. A., & Brinton, D. M. (Eds.). (1997). *The content-based classroom: Perspectives on integrating language and content.* White Plains, NY: Addison-Wesley.

Spolsky, B. (1989). *Conditions for second language learning.* Oxford, UK: Oxford University Press.

State of Wisconsin. (2002). *Alternate performance indicators for limited English proficient students.* Madison: Author.

State of Wisconsin. (2004). *WIDA consortium English language proficiency standards for English language learners in kindergarten through grade 12.* Madison: Author.

Taggart, G. L., Phifer, S. J., Nixon, J. A., & Wood, M. (Eds.). (1998). *Rubrics: A handbook for construction and use.* Lancaster, PA: Technomic.

Teachers of English to Speakers of Other Languages. (1997). *ESL standards for pre-K-12 students.* Alexandria, VA: Author.

Teachers of English to Speakers of Other Languages. (1998). *Managing the assessment process: A framework for measuring student attainment of the ESL standards* (TESOL Professional Papers #5). Alexandria, VA: Author.

Teachers of English to Speakers of Other Languages. (2000, June). *Assessment and accountability of English to speakers of other languages.* Retrieved September 6, 2005, from www.tesol.org/s_tesol/sec_document.asp?CID=32&DID=369

Teachers of English to Speakers of Other Languages. (2001). *Statement on language and literacy development in early childhood for English language learners.* Alexandria, VA: Author.

Teachers of English to Speakers of Other Languages. (2003, March). *Position paper on high-states testing for K-12 English language learners in the United States of America.* Retrieved September 6, 2005, from www.tesol.org/s_tesol/bin.asp?CID=32&DID=375&DOC=FILE.PDF

Thomas, W. P., & Collier, V. P. (2002). *A national study of school effectiveness for language minority students' long-term academic achievement.* Santa Cruz: University of California, Center for Research on Education, Diversity & Excellence.

Thompson, S. J., Johnstone, C. J., & Thurlow, M. L. (2002). *Universal design applied to large scale assessments* (Synthesis Report 44). Minneapolis: University of Minnesota, National Center on Educational Outcomes. Retrieved from the World Wide Web: http://education.umn.edu/NCEO/OnlinePubs/Synthesis44.html

Tinajero, J. V., & Ada, A. F. (Eds.). (1993). *The power of two languages: Literacy and biliteracy for Spanish-speaking students.* New York: Macmillan/McGraw-Hill.

Trumbull, E., & Farr, B. (Eds.). (2000). *Grading and reporting student progress in an age of standards.* Norwood, MA: Christopher-Gordon.

U.S. Department of Education, Office for Civil Rights. (2000). *The use of tests as part of high-stakes decision-making for students: A resource guide for educators and policy-makers.* Washington, DC: Author.

Underhill, N. (1987). *Testing spoken language.* Cambridge, UK: Cambridge University Press.

Wiggins, G. P. (1993). *Assessing student performance.* San Francisco: Jossey-Bass.

Index

Abedi, J., 54, 160, 162
Academic achievement:
  academic language proficiency and, 25–26
  bridging language proficiency and, 31–32
  comparing targets for (chart), 38
  content-based instruction and, 64, 65
  displaying grades for, 173, 176t
  graphic supports for, 137
  measurement for (chart), 99
  standardized testing of, 155, 156–159
    accommodations, 157–159
    alternate assessment, 159
    reporting results, 157, 158t, 160, 161t
    use of multiple measures, 162, 163t
  See also Standards and assessment
Academic content standards:
  bridging language proficiency to, 31–32
  content-based instruction and, 64
  second-language development and, 34–36
  standards-based education and, 90
  See also Standards and assessment
Academic language proficiency:
  academic achievement and, 25–26
  content-based instruction and, 64–65
  reflection on, 66
  social language proficiency and, 24–25
  See also Standards and assessment
Accommodations, 54, 141, 157, 159
Accountability, 63, 160, 162, 164
  See also Standardized testing and reporting
Acquisition process. See Second-language acquisition
Activities, embedded in instruction, 29, 47, 69, 86, 88
Ada, A. F., 49
Ainsworth, L., 141
Alignment, 90, 115
Alternate assessment, 159
American Educational Research Association, 152
Analytic scales, 116, 118–119, 120t
  See also Rubrics for documentation
Ancess, J., 113, 123
Anecdotal records, 44, 52
Arter, J., 117

Ash, G. E., 49
Assessment, 14, 64, 86, 151, 169
  See also specific assessments
Assessment plan, 12, 13t, 21t
Assessment portfolio checklist, 183
Assessment portfolios:
  checklist for, 183
  contents of, 177–179
  family member conferences through, 181–182
  features of, 163, 177
  importance of, 175, 177
  projects and, 88
  reflection on, 178
  teacher-student conferences through, 179–181
  See also Grading systems
Assessment system, components of, 14
August, D., 75, 159
Authenticity, 113

Bachman, L., 9, 24
Bailey, A. L., 41, 170, 172
Baker, D., 46
Bar graphs, 137
Bauman, J. F., 49
Becoming a Nation of Readers, 49
Bell curve, 154
Bilingual education, 3, 4, 64, 160
Biography Self-Assessment, 145t
Brinton, D. M., 41
Brisk, M. E., 55
Brown, H. D., 141
Brumfit, C., 24
Buck, G., 43
Butler, F. A., 41, 157

Calderon, M., 75
Carrasquillo, A. L., 71
Chamot, A. U., 65, 139
Charts, graphs and tables, 68, 136–138
  See also Supports for students
Checklists, 44, 96, 116, 117
  See also Rubrics for documentation
Cheung, A., 51

Christian, D., 51

Christinson, J., 141

Classroom assessment:

constructed responses in, 75, 97, 122

defining tasks and projects for, 88–89

designing, 91–93

content, 91–92

delivery, 94

feedback and use of information, 94

interpreting results, 94

language, 92–93

planning, 91

types of assessment, 93–94

distinctions between, 11–12, 85–86

features of, 89–90

forms of data collection, 95–96

grading and reporting task summary, 109

instructional activities for

listening comprehension, 43–45, 46t

mathematics, 67–70

reading, 51

science, 72–74

social studies, 77–78

speaking, 47–49, 50t

writing, 55–56, 57t

instructional assessment project (sample), 105–108

instructional assessment project (template), 103–104

introduction on, 86–87

measurement for (chart), 99

organization of, 87–88

parameters of (chart), 101

preparation for, 90–91

purposes for (checklist), 19

reflection on, 100

response types in, 96

review sheet (checklist), 102

selected responses in, 96–97

summary and final thoughts on, 97, 98f

Cloze exercises, 96–97

Cohen, A. D., 43

Collier, V. P., 8, 25

Combined model, of self-assessment, 144

Compare and contrast, 134

Conferences, 95, 145, 179–182

Constructed response, 75, 97, 122

Content-based instruction:

features associated with assessment (checklist), 81

introduction on, 64–65

language and

content of mathematics, 65–70

content of science, 71–75

content of social studies, 75–79

nature of, 36, 65

reflections on

approaching math for English language learners, 69

defining language proficiency, 66

multiple meanings, 83

sample listening assessment activity, 82

summary and final thoughts on, 80

Content objectives, 66, 89, 91–92

Content standards. *See* Academic content standards

Content stem, 33

Cooperative learning structures, 76–77, 140

Crandall, J., 67

Criterion-referenced model, of self-assessment, 142–143

Criterion-referenced tests, 87, 152–153

See also Standardized testing and reporting

Cummins, J., 41, 51, 75

Cycles, 136

Darian, S., 71

Darling-Hammond, L., 113, 123

Data collection, 95–96

De Lisi, R., 113

Demographics, 2–3

Designation systems, 116, 157

Developmental rubrics, 121–122

Dietel, R., 160, 162

Differentiating instruction:

by levels of English language proficiency, 34, 47

for scientific inquiry, 73–74, 75

useful tips for, 140–141

Direct observation, 48

Discrete point testing, 43

Dixon, C. N., 55

Documentation. *See* Rubrics for documentation

Dual-language education, 64

Echevarria, J., 65, 139

El Nassar, H., 2

Elementary and Secondary School Act of 2001, 3, 31, 152

Eligibility criteria, 3, 153

Ellison, R., 85

English as a second language (ESL), 3, 4, 64, 160

English language learners:

assessment framework for, 8–9, 10t, 20t

considerations in assessment of, 6

identification of, 6–8

decision tree for placement and (chart), 15

home language survey (checklist), 16

list of measures (checklist), 22

literacy survey (checklist), 18

oral language use survey (checklist), 17

Tier I measures, 7

Tier II measures, 7–8

introduction on, 1–2

large-scale and classroom assessments, 11–12

purposes for assessment of, 8, 9t, 10t, 19t

schedule for assessment of, 12, 13t, 21t

summary and final thoughts on, 12, 13–14

teachers and
definition of English language learners, 3
primary responsibilities, 4–5
reflection on, 5
school demographics, 2–3
English language proficiency:
academic content standards and, 29–36
comparing targets for (chart), 38
English language learners and, 31–32
evaluation checklist for, 40
federal government and, 32–33
measurement of (chart), 99
progress/performance indicators and, 33–34
second-language development and, 34–36
standards-based assessment, 36, 97
academic language functions and, 24
definition of, 3
graphic supports for, 137–138
principles of, 26, 63
See also Oral language development
English language proficiency standards.
See Standards and assessment
English language proficiency testing:
identification and, 7–8
multiple measures of, 162–164, 164t
reporting results of, 159–160, 161t
See also Standardized testing and reporting
English of Speakers of Other Languages
(TESOL), 32, 33, 139
Enright, D. S., 36
ESL (English as a second language), 3, 4, 64
Estrada, P., 73
Evaluation, 86
Ewy, C. A., 134
Extra time, 54

Falk, B., 113, 123
Family member conferences, 181–182
Farr, R., 115, 173, 177, 180
Feedback, 94, 144, 145
Finocchiaro, M., 24
Formative assessments, 51
Fradd, S. H., 155
Freeman, D., 36, 51, 52
Freeman, Y. S., 36, 51, 52

General education program, 58, 64
Genesee, F., 41, 51, 115
Glatthorn, A. A., 113
Glossary textual support, 53, 54
Gómez, E. L., 31, 177
Gottlieb, M., 9, 11, 25, 26, 33, 56, 75,
88, 89, 115, 142, 175
Grade-level equivalents, 154
Grade-level promotion, 153
Grading systems:
assessment portfolios, 175–182
checklist for, 183
contents of, 177–178

family member conferences through,
181–182
features of, 177
reflection on, 178
teacher-student conferences through,
179–181
grading and reporting task summary, 109
introduction on, 169
issues of grading, 169–175
reflections on, 170–171, 173, 176t
the report card,
with same English language proficiency,
170–171
standards-based teaching and learning,
172–173, 174t, 175t
with varying English language proficiency,
171–172
summary and final thoughts on, 182
Graduation, 153
Graphic organizers, 134–136
See also Visual/graphic supports
Graphs, charts, and tables, 68, 136–138
See also Supports for students
Guided reading, 52
Guisbond, L., 124
Guskey, T. R., 88, 113, 170, 172
Gustke, C., 115

Hakuta, K., 159
Halliday, M. A. K., 24
Hamayan, E., 26
Harrington, M. M., 55
Haug, C. A., 54
Hein, G. E., 71, 115
High-stake testing, 65, 152
Hill, B. C., 49
Histograms, 137
Holistic scales, 53, 119, 121, 122t
Homan, S. P., 52
Home language survey (checklist), 16
Hyerle, D., 134
Hymes, D. H., 43

Identification process, 6–8
decision tree for placement and (chart), 15
home language survey (checklist), 16
list of measures (checklist), 22
literacy survey (checklist), 18
oral language use survey (checklist), 17
Tier I measures, 7
Tier II measures, 7–8
Improving America's School Act of 1994, 31
Individualized education plan (IEP), 141, 159
Information gathering, self-assessment as,
144–145
Instructional assessment cycle, 90, 98f
Instructional supports:
acquisition and learning strategies, 139–140
interaction with partners, 76–77, 94, 140

for social studies, 77–78
teacher input, 139
See also Supports for students
Interactive support, 140
See also Cooperative learning structures
Interdisciplinary project (sample), 128–130
International Reading Association (IRA),
31, 51, 152
Interviews, 95

Johnstone, C. J., 141

Kamé enui, E. J., 49
Kamii, C., 152
Katz, A., 170
Kessler, C., 71
Khruschchev, N., 151
Kindler, A. L., 2
Kiplinger, V. L., 54
KLWH strategy, 144
Krashen, S. D., 26, 43

L1 (native language), 3, 4, 27, 51
L2 (second language), 51
Language domains, 9, 24, 42, 78, 92, 160
Language functions, 24, 45, 69, 92, 117
Language objectives, 44, 65–66, 92
Language patterns, 136
Language proficiency standards.
See Standards and assessment
Language tests, 152
Large-scale assessment:
accommodations for, 54, 141, 157, 159
checklist for analyzing features of, 60–61
classroom measures and, 11–12, 87, 88
content-based instruction and, 65
differentiating instruction and, 140–141
features of classroom assessment and, 149
instructional activities for
listening comprehension, 45
mathematics, 70
reading, 53–54
science, 74–75
social studies, 77–79
speaking, 48–49, 50t
writing, 57–58
measurement for (chart), 99
National Assessment of Educational
Progress (NAEP), 147
types of student responses in, 96
Lawton, T. A., 155
Learning logs, 144–145
Learning strategies, 139–140
Levels of language proficiency:
content objectives and, 92–93
differentiating instruction by, 34
grouping by levels of language proficiency
(chart), 27, 39

instructional assessment ideas by, 29, 30t
issues of grading
the report card, 173, 176t
with same English language proficiency,
170–171
standards-based teaching and learning,
172–173, 174t, 175t
with varying English language proficiency,
171–172
reflection on, 27
second-language acquisition process and,
27, 28t
specificity of vocabulary use, 74
Limited English proficient, 3
Linguistic supports. *See* Supports for students
Listening comprehension:
classroom assessment of, 43–45, 46t
large-scale assessment of, 45
nature of, 42–43
sample assessment activity, 82
See also Oral language development
Literacy dependent, 78, 155
Literacy development:
acquisition and learning strategies, 139–140
connecting oral language with, 55, 59t
introduction on, 41–42
reading comprehension
classroom assessment of, 51–53
large-scale assessment of, 53–54
nature of, 49, 51
reflection on, 52
summary and final thoughts on, 58
writing
classroom assessment for, 55–56, 57t
large-scale assessment of, 57–58
nature of, 55
See also Oral language development
Literacy survey (checklist), 18
Long, R., 36

Madsen, H. S., 43
Manipulatives, 45, 68, 72, 78
Manning, G., 36
Manning, M., 36
Mathematics content, assessing
language and, 65–70
See also Content-based instruction
Matrix. *See* Rubrics for documentation
McCloskey, M. L., 36
McGee, P. L., 155
McTighe, J., 117
Modifications, 141, 157, 159
Mohan, B., 41, 65, 71
Multidisciplinary units, 69
Multimedia entries, in assessment
portfolios, 179
Multiple measures (data sources):
of academic achievement, 162–164

assessment and, 86, 123, 152
   schedule for assessment and, 12, 13*t*, 21*t*
   types of measures (checklist), 19
Murphy, S., 88

Narrative forms, of self-assessment, 144–145
Nation, I. S. P., 49
National Assessment of Educational Progress
   (NAEP), 147
National Association for the Education of Young
   Children, 51
National Center for Educational Statistics
   (NCES), 147
National Center for Fair and Open Testing, 152
National Council of Teachers of English (NCTE),
   21, 152
National Council of Teachers of Mathematics
   (NCTM), 31, 152
National Education Association, 152
National Reading Panel, 49
National Research Council, 31, 71
Native language (L1), 3, 4, 27, 51
Navarrete, C. J., 115, 177
Needs assessment survey, 118
Neill, M., 124
Nessel, D., 55
Newton, I., 63
Nixon, J. A., 115
No Child Left Behind Act of 2001 (NCLB),
   3, 31, 152, 159
Norm-referenced tests, 87, 152–155
   See also Standardized testing and reporting
Normal curve equivalents, 154
Numbered heads together, 77

Observation checklists, 163
O'Malley, J. M., 45, 65, 115, 139, 141, 179
On Our Way to English, 51
Oral language development:
   acquisition and learning strategies, 139–140
   connecting literacy with, 55, 59*t*
   introduction on, 41–42
   listening comprehension
      classroom assessment of, 43–45, 46*t*
      large-scale assessment of, 45
      nature of, 42–43
      sample assessment activity, 82
   measures of accountability for, 164
   speaking
      classroom assessment of, 47–48
      large-scale assessment of, 48–49, 50*t*
      nature of, 45–47
   summary and final thoughts on, 58
Oral language use survey (checklist), 17
Oral reports, 145, 146*t*

Paper-and-pencil tasks, 74
Pardo, E. B., 51

Paris, S. G., 155
Peer assessment, 76, 94, 145–146
Percentiles, 153
Performance assessments:
   importance of, 113–114
   interdisciplinary project (sample), 128–130
   nature of, 87, 95, 112, 113*t*
   rationale for, 111–112
   rubrics for documentation, 114–125
      checklist of rubric features, 131
      modifying rubrics, 116
      overall features of, 123, 145
      reflections on matching instruction to
         assessment, 126
      types and purposes of, 3, 44, 116–125
      types of rubrics, 127
      useful applications, 50*t*, 115–116
   standardized testing and, 152
   summary and final thoughts on, 123–124
Performance/progress indicators:
   English language proficiency standards and,
      33–34
   for listening, 44, 45*t*
   for scientific inquiry, 73–74
   for speaking, 48
Phifer, S. J., 115
Pie charts, 137
Pierce, L. V., 45, 51, 115, 141
Pitino, R., 23
Portfolios. *See* Assessment portfolios
Price, S., 71, 115
Productive language, 26
Progress/performance indicators:
   English language proficiency standards and,
      33–34
   for listening, 44, 45*t*
   for scientific inquiry, 73–74
   for speaking, 48
Projects, embedded in instruction, 69, 86, 88–89

Quinn, M. E., 71
Quizzes, 95

Rating scales, 48, 94, 116, 118, 142
Raw scores, 153
Reading comprehension:
   classroom assessment of, 51–53
   large-scale assessment of, 53–54
   nature of, 49, 51
   reflection on, 52
   See also Literacy development
Receptive language, 26
Reclassification, 153
Reflective model, of self-assessment, 143–144
Reliability, 3, 97, 113
Report cards, 173, 176*t*
Reporting results, on standardized tests.
      See Standardized testing and reporting

Résumé Self-Assessment Questions, 144t
Rhodes, L. K., 52
Richard-Amato, P. A., 177
Rivera, C., 157
Rodríguez, V., 71
Role play, 45
Roth, J. L., 155
Round robin, 77
Rubrics for documentation, 114–123
    checklist of rubric features, 131
    overall features of, 88, 123, 145
    reflections on
        matching instruction to assessment, 126
        modifying rubrics, 116
        types of rubrics, 127
    types and purposes of, 3, 44, 116–125
        analytic scales, 116, 118–119, 120t
        checklists, 44, 96, 116, 117
        holistic scales, 53, 119, 121, 122t
        rating scales, 48, 94, 116, 118, 142
        task-specific scales, 121–123, 124t, 125t
    useful applications, 50t, 115–116
    See also Performance assessments

Sacks, P., 152
Scaffolding instruction, 139
Schaeffer, B., 124
Scialdone, L., 157
Science content, assessing language and, 71–75
    See also Content-based instruction
Scientific inquiry, 71
Scoring guides, rubrics for documentation
Second-language acquisition:
    academic content standards and, 34–36
    continuum marking, 26–29
        instructional assessment ideas, 29, 30t
        levels of language proficiency, 27, 28t
        reflection on, 27
        types of support, 27–28, 29t
    language proficiency standards and, 33–34
Second language development.
        See Second-language acquisition
Selected response, 96–97, 159
Self-assessment, 76, 94, 141
    See also Student self-assessment
Semantic webs, 136
Shanklin, N. L., 52
Shared reading, 51
Shared-to-guided reading, 51
Sharkey, M., 157
Shearer, A. P., 52
Shohamy, E., 152
Short, D. J., 41, 65, 139
Slavin, R. E., 51
Smith, J. K., 113
Smith, L. F., 113
Smith, M., 71
Snow, M. A., 177

Social language proficiency, 24–25, 58
Social studies content, assessing language and,
    75–79
    See also Content-based instruction
Speaking:
    classroom assessment of, 47–48
    large-scale assessment of, 48–49, 50t
    nature of, 45–47
    See also Oral language development
Speech components, 46
Standard scores, 154, 157
Standardized testing and reporting:
    comparison of features (chart), 167
    English language learners and, 155–164
        accountability for, 160, 162
        identification and, 7–8
        standardized language proficiency testing,
            159–160, 161t
        testing of academic achievement, 155,
            156–159
        use of multiple measures, 162–164
    introduction on, 3, 151
    norm-referenced achievement tests
        (chart), 166
    reflections on
        information on standardized tests, 155
        matching instructional modifications to
            accommodations, 157
    standardized tests
        appropriateness debate over, 152
        norm-referenced and criterion-referenced,
            152–153
        use of data from, 153–155
    summary and final thoughts on, 164–165
Standards and assessment:
    content-based instruction and, 64–65
    introduction on, 23
    language proficiency and academic content
        standards, 29–36
        comparing targets for (chart), 38
        English language learners and, 31–32
        evaluation checklist for, 40
        federal government and, 32–33
        progress/performance indicators, 33–34
        second-language development and, 33,
            34–36
        standards-based assessment, 36, 97
    relationships among, 24–26
        academic language proficiency and
            academic achievement, 25–26
        social and academic language functions, 24
        social and academic language proficiency,
            24–25
    second-language acquisition process, 26–29
        grouping by levels of language proficiency
            (chart), 27, 39
        instructional assessment ideas and, 29, 30t
        levels of language proficiency and, 27, 28t

reflection on, 27
   types of support for English language
      learners, 27–28, 29t
   summary and final thoughts on, 36–37
   traditional grading practices and, 172–173
   See also Standardized testing and reporting
Standards-based assessment, 36, 97
Stanines, 153
Stansfield, C. W., 157
Stevens, R. A., 157
Storytelling self-assessment (checklist), 143t
Strand of performance, 34, 44
Student reflection. See Student self-assessment
Student self-assessment:
   combined model of, 144
   criterion-referenced model of, 142–143
   as information gathering and feedback, 144–145
   introduction on, 141–142
   reflective model of, 143–144
   See also Supports for students
Student-teacher conferences, 95, 145, 179–181
Study skills, 139
Summative assessment, 151
Supports for students:
   differentiating instruction, 140–141
   features of classroom/large-scale
      assessment, 149
   features of graphic organizers, 148
   forms of visual/graphic support,
      77–78, 134–138
      charts, graphs, and tables, 68, 136–138
      graphic organizers, 134–136
   instructional supports, 138–140
      acquisition and learning strategies,
         139–140
      interaction with partners, 76–77, 94, 140
      for mathematics, 67–68
      for social studies, 77–78
      teacher input, 139
   introduction on, 133–134
   National Assessment of Educational Progress
      (NAEP), 147
   peer assessment, 76, 94, 145–146
   student self-assessment, 141–145
      combined model of, 144
      criterion-referenced model of, 142–143
      as information gathering and feedback,
         144–145
      reflective model of, 143–144
   summary and final thoughts on, 147
   types of linguistic supports, 27–28, 29t, 53, 94

T-charts, 136
Tables, charts, and graphs, 68, 136–138
   See also Supports for students
Taggart, G. L., 115
Task analyses, 47
Task-specific scales, 121–123, 124t, 125t

Tasks, embedded in instruction, 86, 88–89
Teacher observation, 95–96
Teacher responsibilities, 4–5
Teacher-student conferences, 95, 145, 179–181
Teachers of English to Speakers of Other
   Languages, 51, 152
Technology, 93–94
Terrell, T. D., 26
TESOL (English to Speakers of Other
   Languages), 32, 33, 139
Test-taking skills, 139–140
Tests/testing, 85–86, 95, 152
Think-aloud activities, 47
Think-pair-share, 76–77
Thomas, W. P., 8, 25
Thompson, S. J., 141
Thurlow, M. L., 141
Tier I measures, 7
Tier II measures, 7–8
Timelines, 78
Tinajero, J. V., 49, 51
Title I, 4
Tone, B., 115, 180
Trumbull, E., 115, 173, 177
Turner, J. C., 155
Twain, M., 111
Two-way task, 47, 76

U. S. Census Bureau, 2
U. S. Department of Education's Office
   for Civil Rights, 152
Underhill, N., 45
Underwood, T., 88
Universal test design, 141
Upshur, J. A., 115

Validity, 3, 113, 156
Venn Diagrams, 134, 136
Visual/graphic supports:
   charts, graphs, and tables, 68, 136–138
   content of social studies and, 77–78
   features of graphic organizers, 148
   graphic organizers, 134–136
   See also Supports for students
Vocabulary development, 49, 73
Vogt, M. E., 65, 139

Wiggins, G. P., 113
Winfrey, O., 1, 169
Wood, M., 115
World-Class Instructional Design and
   Assessment Consortium (WIDA), 160, 161t
Writing:
   classroom assessment for, 55–56, 57t
   large-scale assessment of, 57–58
   nature of, 55
   See also Literacy development
Writing portfolio, 56

**CORWIN
PRESS**

The Corwin Press logo—a raven striding across an open book—represents the union of courage and learning. Corwin Press is committed to improving education for all learners by publishing books and other professional development resources for those serving the field of PreK–12 education. By providing practical, hands-on materials, Corwin Press continues to carry out the promise of its motto: **"Helping Educators Do Their Work Better."**